Tales from the Middle Border

Tales from the Middle Border

Richard Quinney

Borderland Books

Copyright ©2007 Richard Quinney

All rights reserved. No part of this book may be reproduced in any form without written permission from the publisher, with the exception of brief excerpts for review purposes.

Published by Borderland Books, Madison, WI
www.borderlandbooks.net

Publisher's Cataloging-in-Publication Data
Quinney, Richard.
  Tales from the middle border / Richard Quinney — 1st ed.
    p. : ill. ; cm.
    Includes bibliographical references.

ISBN: 978-0-9768781-3-1

1. Quinney, Richard 2. Quinney, Richard — Homes and Haunts — Wisconsin — Walworth County.
3. Sociologists — United States — Biography.
4. Farm Life — Wisconsin — Walworth County.
5. Wisconsin — Biography. I. Title.
CT275.Q554 A3 2007
977/.5043/092   2006901464

Printed in the United States of America
First edition

Whether by chance or fate or accident,
The truth is this, the cut fell to the Knight,
Which everybody greeted with delight,
And tell his tale he must, as reason was
Because our agreement and because
He too had sworn. What more is there to say?

>   Geoffrey Chaucer, *The Canterbury Tales*

In the autumn when the wind swept through the bare branches of the elm, I thought of the lonely days of plowing on the prairie, and the poetry and significance of those wild gray days came over me with such power that I instinctively seized my pen to write of them.

>   Hamlin Garland, *A Son of the Middle Border*

Contents

Prologue ix

A Place Called Home 1

Lodging for the Night 43

A Traveler of Country Roads 61

A Winter's Tale 77

The Loneliest Sound Is the Whistle of a Train 91

Once My Father Traveled West to California 111

My Mother's Diary 135

I Am Native to This 157

List of Photographs 177

Bibliography 179

Prologue

LIKE THE KNIGHT in Geoffrey Chaucer's *Canterbury Tales,* whether by chance or fate or accident, I drew the shortest cut, and I have told the tales that I had sworn to tell. We are pilgrims on a journey, traveling through the middle border of a vast continent. We tell stories to each other along the way, finding solace in our common travel. We wish to live our lives with deliberation, giving attention to the wonders of our everyday existence. We know that our farthest travel is to the place where we started.

The common theme that runs through these tales — these tales in the form of the personal essay — is that of setting forth and returning. Autobiographical reflection allows the narrator to move in time and through space, tracing a life from an early time to a later one, and interpreting a life as it moves across a geographical landscape. The act of writing is to document and to understand the travel that may result in a homecoming.

"Memory is a kind of accomplishment," wrote the poet William Carlos Williams, "a sort of renewal." In reconstructing my life—through the memory that comes with writing—I gain some understanding of the person I have become. The remembered past becomes my present reality. Hamlin Garland wrote of his Midwest life, recalled in the process of writing: "Some say it is all illusion, this world of memory, or imagination, but to me the remembered past is more and more the reality." The impulse to write autobiographically is to know the present and, at the same time, to apprehend what is yet to be. The teller of tales is finding a place within which to dwell, and some rest is found in the telling. We tell our stories to save and to renew our lives.

Going home can take us forward to what might and could be, rather than backward to something that never was. We return home to find our place in the world. We cease to be wanderers once we have started the journey home. The farm in Wisconsin forever furnishes me with the image of what is home. It is that concrete and visible place, a deeply loved place, which draws me to the wonders of this life. Throughout these tales is the sense that everything extraordinary is grounded first in ordinary experience. As storytellers, we are witnesses to the qualities of everyday life.

There is no retirement in this life. Even in times of illness, especially in such times, life continues with a sense of the sublime and a renewed appreciation of the details of daily life. In my case, writing a few careful words holds a life together and gives meaning to the day. I have the hope that these words—these tales I have sworn to tell—will be of help and solace to others. Unceasingly, we continue our explorations along the middle border.

THESE PERSONAL ESSAYS—these tales—were written over a period of several years. With the exception of my story of growing up on the farm, the essays were written as they were being lived. In the making of this book, I have revised the essays, some extensively. I acknowledge the permissions granted to me by the publishers of my books *Journey to a Far Place, For the Time Being, Borderland,* and *Where Yet the Sweet Birds Sing.*

I welcome the opportunity to tell the stories of a lifetime. Like the Ancient Mariner, I never cease to tell—and to reshape—my stories. Finally, and most importantly, I acknowledge with gratitude all the friends, family members, and passing strangers who have been part of these stories. I know the good fortune of the storyteller.

A Place Called Home

A LONG TIME AGO, after the blowing of mighty winds and the creation of a universe, a planet that we would come to call Earth began to orbit one of the suns in the galaxy Milky Way. A great sheet of ice eventually moved slowly southward, cutting and dredging and leaving deposits of rock and soil and making the rolling hills of southern Wisconsin. Rivers and creeks flowed through the fertile land. Fish swam in the waters and muskrats built their houses on the ponds that lay at the foot of the gently sloping hills. Red-winged blackbirds returned each spring to the marshes, and cowslips sprang up among the bogs. Red-tailed hawks soared all summer long above the giant oak trees. In winter, snow covered the ground, and all was still except for an occasional field mouse making its way from one place to another.

There were people on this land before the coming of the settlers. The settlers that came to Walworth County displaced the Chippewa, the Ottawa, and the Potawatomi. They were forced from their native land and moved to areas west of the Mississippi. The land was settled by Irish emigrants fleeing the potato famine in the 1840s. This is the place that continues to be my home.

My earliest memory is of my grandfather coming across the field from the old place to help with the morning chores. I remember my father saying, "Here comes the old man." John Quinney's parents had come to this country from County Kilkenny in Ireland. John's father, whose name also was John, sailed from Ireland to New York in 1849, three years after Bridget O'Keefe had immigrated to the United States from County Kilkenny. Both John and Bridget settled in Yonkers, married, and while living in Yonkers Bridget gave birth to two of their five children. The lure of farmland and new life in Wisconsin inspired them to move by steamboat up the Hudson, through the Erie Canal, across the Great Lakes to Milwaukee, and finally to the village of Millard in Walworth County, sixty miles west of Lake Michigan. There they rented a farm until they earned enough by 1868 to purchase the thirty acres for the homestead. The site is still called "the old place."

Bridget, who lived forty years past the death of John, is pictured in a family album sitting by the lilac bushes in front of the white frame house smoking an Irish clay pipe. My father would tell us stories about how she and the other Irish farm women would gather on Monday mornings to wash and rinse the week's clothes along the sandbar that jutted out from the muskrat pond across the field.

John and Bridget's daughter Kate, who worked as a dressmaker and seamstress, lived all her life at the old place. Their son Tom left the homestead for South Dakota when he was young and settled on a small farm eight miles south of Alexandria after the government opened the land for settlement west of the Missouri. A few years later Bill, Tom's brother, also made his way to South Dakota where he settled on a farm until moving into town. When Bill died, his obituary notice, mailed back to Wisconsin, stated that he was "possessed of a friendly disposition" and that he was "well liked by all who knew him." John and Bridget's youngest child, daughter Mary, lived her entire life within fifteen miles of her birthplace. She married Henry Reynolds, and they farmed on the edge of Lake Como. A photograph shows them with farm neighbors and relatives gathered beneath a huge oak tree for the wedding of their daughter. Mary and Henry's son Howard, at the auctioning of the Reynolds farm in the 1940s, an event that marked an end to Howard's lifetime of farming, gave me a riding horse named Lady. The prettiest horse ever found on a farm, Lady had been trained to neck rein and to run the smoothest of gaits, the single-foot.

My father's father, John, son of John and Bridget, married Hattie Reynolds of nearby Rock County shortly before the turn of the century. Hattie died a few years later of consumption, leaving John with two daughters, Marjorie and Nellie, and a son, Floyd. A year after her mother's death, little Nellie died at the age of eighteen months. John Quinney never remarried. Floyd would tell his own sons what the old man had always told him: "I could never find another woman who would be as good to my children as Hattie was."

Yellowing photographs show my father's sister Marjorie standing in long dresses in the yard at the old place. For most of her short life, Marjorie worked as a maid in the houses and cottages of the wealthy families who vacationed around Delavan Lake. Only years later, after Marjorie's death at the age of forty, did my father reveal that she had owned and operated a tavern a few miles southwest of Delavan during the last years of her life. Wherever I have lived after leaving the farm, I have kept a framed picture of Marjorie on top of my bookcase.

My father, Floyd Quinney, was born at the dawn of the twentieth century, in the year 1900. His birthday came in March as the Wisconsin winter was beginning to show signs of breaking. He farmed all his life, adding a few acres through the years to increase the size of the farm. He had worked for a short period during his teen years and early twenties as a weaver in the Delavan knitting mills. There he had learned a knitter's knot, one so small and tight that it could pass through a machine's needle. Years later, with great pride, he taught the knitter's knot to his sons.

As a young man, I heard tales of my father's youth and good times. He had owned one of the first Model Ts in Sugar Creek Township. After the harvest in the fall of 1924, he and his good friend Marvin Kittlesen set out in the Ford for California. They worked along the way to pay their expenses, finally hooking up with a California Power and Light Company crew to build towers for high-power electricity. The two were home for the spring planting. The images of their trip remain stored in the veneer music cabinet on the front porch of the farmhouse. After the Second World War, my father occasionally talked about selling out and opening a hamburger shop in town, something that would put him in Delavan and in contact with other people.

My mother, Alice Marie, grew up on a farm north of Millard, as the only child of William Holloway and Lorena Taylor. In an old photograph she stands alone on a snow-covered hill beside the South Side Heart Prairie School. Her mother died of Bright's disease when she was fifteen years old. After graduating from high school in Elkhorn, she attended the nine-month course in rural education at the State Normal School in Whitewater. She then taught for five years the eight grades at Bay Hill School near Williams Bay. It was during these school-teaching years that she met the man that would become my father at a dance one night in Delavan. They married the following year, in 1930. I was born in 1934, and my brother Ralph was born two years later. Our family was now complete.

My mother's family was English on both sides. Her maternal great-grandfather, George Taylor, was a cabinetmaker and carpenter who designed and built several handsome Greek Revival farmhouses that still stand in LaGrange Township. On her father's side, the Holloways had been tenant farmers on a lord's estate in Devon. James

Holloway, my mother's grandfather, emigrated to America and eventually bought the farm north of Millard, and as the obituary of 1911 says, "by diligence and hard labor made it a fine place."

My grandfather, W. V. B. Holloway, was regarded early in his life as one of the most progressive of Sugar Creek's younger farmers. He held the elective position of township clerk for fifty-six years. I remember my grandfather arguing with Julius Johnson, one of Sugar Creek's few Democrats, late into the night about Roosevelt's New Deal.

Later in his life, Will, as everyone called him, would sit at his desk in his house working on township business. In a photograph published by the *Elkhorn Enterprise* to accompany an article commemorating his many years of clerking for Sugar Creek, he is shown sitting at his desk, a plat map of the county stretched out in front of him. A rubber band is holding up the sleeve of his dress shirt, and a visor, worn to shield the light from the lamp, rests on the desk. A wooden telephone, with two bells on top and a pencil on a string dangling from the voice piece, hangs on the wall behind him. Each evening, he walked to the corner store in Millard to pick up the newspaper. As he walked home at dusk one February evening, in his eighty-sixth year, he was struck and killed in front of his house by a passing driver.

My father and mother continued to farm into the last years of the 1960s. The nature of farming changed rapidly in their later years. As they got older and their sons moved away, they gradually reduced their farm work, avoiding the expensive changes that would have been required. My father died of a heart attack while repairing the tractor on a cold November day. My mother continued to live alone on the farm until passing away as she neared her ninety-third year.

As a child, I sensed that I was an intimate part of the landscape. The woods and fields and sky measured the depth and breadth of my existence. Standing on a hill, I would look toward the far ridges and know the immensity of the world. The landscape of the farm has been a source of inspiration all of my life.

One day, when I was eight years old, I walked along the cow path east of the barn, on the side of the hill that ran down to the woods. I lay down on my back in the pasture grass and looked up into the sky. Coming out of the clouds, in many colors, appeared an image—the face of George Washington. I was struck with surprise and then with awe. It occurred to me that I had been singled out for something special. Good works must follow this privileged experience. I felt that I had been chosen.

This mysterious feeling of wonder and purpose was part of my early years in the country school. Dunham School, District Number 9, was a one-room building of red brick that stood on an acre of land surrounded by large silver maples and American elms. The girls' outhouse was along the south fence in back of the school, the boys' outhouse, to the north. A baseball diamond occupied the rest of the yard. Looking out toward the west, beyond the fields and woods, I could see the farm. Inside the one-room school, a world was being created.

Getting to school in the morning and returning home at the end of the day were part of the adventure of school. Most days of the year, my brother Ralph and I either walked or rode our bicycles to school. When walking, we took the gravel road, the longer distance, or we would cut across the fields and through the woods. The family album contains photographs taken the first day of each school year. We are poised at our bicycles, sometimes with one leg thrown over the bar, ready for the ride to school.

Halfway up the winding road, we stopped each morning to pick up the Gies kids, Betty and Jim. From there on, the journey to school was affected by the seasons of the year. On bright fall days, the last of the goldenrod and sumac marked our way. Later, migrating ducks and geese made their calls flying overhead. In early spring, following the long winter, water flowed beneath cracking ice and hardened snow along the sides of the road. One year in late spring, we sang all the way to school, "Oh what a beautiful morning."

Winter furnished us with the greatest adventures of travel to and from school. There were days of walking in knee-deep snow, and arduous journeys through the stark, silent woods. The highlight of travel was to ride the bobsleigh. A snowfall of two or three feet meant that the milkman would not be able to make it down the road to the farm. Our father would have to get the cans of milk up to the main road, a distance of over a mile. He would hitch the two white workhorses to the long bobsleigh and would load in the milk cans. Ralph and I would pile in; our father, dressed in his wool-lined coat, would take the reins, and with the breath steaming from the horses' nostrils, we would make our way to the main road. We often had to stop to shovel our way through the deep drifts. On other days, if the snowplow had already cleared the road, we would glide over the packed snow with great style in the one-horse sleigh, bells ringing all the way to school.

Arriving at school, we placed our winter coats and boots in the front vestibule, put our lunch pails on the shelf, and sometimes, before sitting down to work, made a treat for our winter lunch, snow mousse. Into a metal container we poured a mixture of sugar, chocolate syrup, eggs and cream, and then buried the container outside in the snow. At noon the mousse would be ready for dessert.

And then one morning, spring would finally come to Dunham School. Skeeter Duesterbeck, pulling a wagon by hand, would come down the road with a can of fresh drinking water for the day. Pat McDonald and I, being assigned the daily task, would run the flag up the pole in the front yard of the school. We would settle into our desks, placing books and tablets in the compartments under the desktops. Throughout the day, each grade, consisting of two or three students, would take its turn as a class in the front of the room. The rest of us continued with our studies, listening much of the time to our teacher, Miss Roeker, and to our friends reciting their lessons. We learned from those who were younger, at a point where we had once been, and from those who were older and more advanced in their studies. Eight grades of students were learning together.

During those years, at 10:30 every Monday morning, the teacher turned on the radio to WHA, the state educational station in Madison. This was the morning for "Afield with Ranger Mac." Wakelin McNeel, with all the wonder in his voice, broadcast this program on the Wisconsin School of the Air for twenty years to children in the rural schools. "Come along, boys and girls," he would say, and "the trail hitters" would be off with Ranger Mac, exploring the marshes, walking the edge of a farm creek, or entering a northern pine forest. We learned about the earth's natural resources and the changing signs of the seasons and the intimate joys of being attuned to the world of nature. Ranger Mac ended each program: "And until next week, may the Great Spirit put sunshine in your heart today and forever more, heap much."

In the back of the schoolroom was the museum. An oak cabinet with glass doors, it contained the artifacts of nature and the wonders of earthly habitation. Collected on walks to and from school were Indian arrowheads, snake skins, the skull of a skunk, all kinds of rocks, jars of powdery substances, large mushrooms, strangely shaped twigs, a turtle shell, and decaying objects gathered long ago but too precious to discard. Years later, I wondered what had happened to the specimens after Dunham School had closed for the last time in the 1950s, a casualty of school consolidation.

Two recesses a day, plus the noon hour, gave us time for play. Fall and spring were times for baseball games, boys and girls teaming together on a baseball field well worn from seventy-five years of play. The old merry-go-round turned most of the time during recess, sometimes swinging back and forth until it nearly fell off its center pole. Dividing into sides, we played Andy-Over-the-School-House, tagging each other to increase our team size as the game progressed. One warm spring day, with the smell of peanut butter and jam sandwiches still hanging in the noontime air, we built a grass house over fallen branches. Some older students later boasted about doing unusual things in the darkness of the grass house.

One particularly cold and dark March afternoon, we were skating on the pond beyond the fence in the field of the Duesterbeck farm. Suddenly I yelled across the ice to Bob Duesterbeck, who was making a turn on the other side of the pond: "Bob loves Pearl!" This immediately caught Bob's attention. He skated toward me at a fast clip and threw me down on the ice. My leg broke sharply in two places. Carefully tended by my mother, I spent the next six weeks at home on the sofa. On dark winter days for years to come, my aching leg reminded me of Bob and Pearl and the love I attributed to them.

The following winter provided us with a memorable Christmas program. The schoolroom was lavishly decorated with a colored Nativity scene chalked on the blackboard and construction paper figures pinned to the wallboard around the room. At the completion of the evening's

Christmas program of stories, skits, recitations, and musical numbers, Santa Claus appeared with the slam of the front door and the ringing of sleigh bells. We, students and adults, knew that the year's Santa was the farmer up the road from the school, the man who drank too much. After handing out the presents, Santa concluded his lively appearance by engaging both the young and old in a contest. With the room divided in half, he instructed everyone to see which side could sing "Silent Night" louder. The irony of the event was not lost on anyone by the time the shouting neared its end. Into the winter night we went with "Silent Night" literally ringing in our ears.

Following the spring planting and before the beginning of the summer haying season, the annual Dunham School picnic marked the end of the school year. Before the picnic dinner began, students and adults together enjoyed a game of baseball, while the old-timers reminisced in small groups around the schoolyard. I was busy taking around the autograph book that I had started during the school year, trying to get each page filled by the end of the day. My classmate Mary Balogh presented me with an autograph that read: "You had a little lamp, very well trained no doubt. Every time your girlfriend comes, the little lamp goes out." Ending the verse, she added, "Yours till Niagara Falls." Jimmy Gies wrote, "When you see a monkey up in a tree, just pull his tail and think of me." Our neighbor Burton Hanson wrote, "Remember me when far, far off, where the woodchucks die with the whooping cough."

During one of her visits to the school in 1946, the country school superintendent, Ella Jacobson, summarized what learning meant for me, both at Dunham School and in subsequent years when learning became not only my work but also my happiness: "Every time I visit this school I find you doing good work. Always do your very best in everything you do. This will bring you success, and you will be happy in your work."

In the spring of 1947, at the end of my seventh grade, only five students remained at Dunham School. The school had to be closed until there were more students. I completed the eighth grade at Island School in Richmond Township. Ralph and I walked west through fields and woods to reach the school. That year, for the first time in my life, I felt the painful reality of change. The transfer to Island School marked the beginning of a move from home.

I liked my eighth-grade teacher, Miss Helling. But social relations with other students took on a new character. There was competitiveness in playing with others that I had not previously known. Baseball games had become a test of one's strength and athletic ability. Play was now a threatening experience, and I was bewildered and overwhelmed when another boy asked an unheard-of question: "Why don't you show me yours?"

The eighth grade finally drew to an end. I was selected from candidates from all the grade schools in Richmond Township to deliver the commencement speech. At the countywide commencement, held in Lake Geneva, I carefully prepared a speech on the early settlers of Richmond Township. As I began to speak, dressed in new trousers and my first sport coat, my trousers began to darken. In excitement and fear I had wet my pants.

AFTER A SUMMER of working in the fields, I began high school. The four years of Delavan High School marked a period of departure from the life of the farm. I never completed the leave-taking, although I lived those years trying to move away from the farm, believing that I had to sever all ties to the ways of life on the farm. Removing the farm from my life would never be possible, but as a teenager, I did not know this.

Although I had not reached the legal driving age when I began high school, I obtained a special driver's permit, and my parents allowed me to use the pickup truck to drive the five miles to the high school. Driving into town in the truck and searching for a parking space near the school let everyone know that I was from the farm. My clothes had the look of country, although I tried to dress like the town kids. On my mind much of the time was the difference between the students who had grown up in town and those who had grown up on the farm. But rather than define my rural background with some distinction and pride, I accepted the assigned second-class citizenship and tried to become more like the town students.

During the second year in high school, my difficulties in making the transition to town became more acute.

I developed sharp stomach pains that made getting to school a trial each morning. The pain finally settled on the right side: the obvious sign of appendicitis. Dr. Crowe agreed with my persistent self-diagnosis. The appendix must come out. Following the operation, the doctor placed the appendix in a jar and studied it. There was no inflammation; he had removed a perfectly good appendix. But I began to feel better, and after the operation and recovery, I returned to school with new confidence.

I threw myself into extracurricular activities to prove my worth both to myself and to others. My classes were going well, but I noticed that students became known by their accomplishments outside class. Sports were out for me; I lacked the skills that come with years of practice, and besides, I had to get home after school to do chores on the farm. Instead, I became the photographer for the high school newspaper. I photographed school events, football and basketball games, plays, and teachers, and made candid shots in the hallways. On stormy nights, I traveled to Lake Geneva, Walworth, and McHenry to cover the games. With Lee Farrar and Terry Itnyre, I wrote the stories, finding twenty-five different verbs, including "whips," "trounces," "bows to," and "licks," to headline the results of a game, and carefully avoiding verbs like "wins" and "defeats." I learned to develop and print film, and each week one of my photographs appeared on the front page of the *Spotlight*.

I received a good review for my part in "The Ugly Duckling." "He shows promise," the reviewer in the town newspaper wrote. It was my first and last part in a play; but during the months of rehearsal, I had gotten to know the town students better. And they had begun to pay some attention to me. The high point for me came when Bill Hodge invited me to come to his house with other town kids to watch General MacArthur on television deliver his "old soldiers never die" speech to the United States Congress. I surely was beginning to make it in town.

At the start of my first year of high school, I decided that I would play in the high school band. I selected the trombone, and though I had never held one before, I knew it was the right instrument for me. With some of the money received from raising pigs, I purchased a new silver trombone. It went with me through college, where I also played in the band. In graduate school and in my second year of marriage, I took the trombone to the radio store near the state capitol in Madison and told the dealer that I wanted to trade it for an FM radio. The dealer said, "Are you certain you want to do this? You'll never have the money to buy another trombone." And for a long time, he was right.

I learned to play the trombone in lessons given to me by Mr. Kleyensteuber, the band director. Soon I was in the band among the trombones. The band marched at the games, put on concerts, and made trips throughout southeastern Wisconsin. In the clarinet section sat Peggy Starin, who became my high school sweetheart. Peggy followed me to college the year after I graduated from high school. With my sights on graduate school and an uncertain career, and Peggy desiring a more dependable partner, we parted forever.

During my third year in high school, I formed a band that played at school dances. On one occasion, with crepe paper streamers hanging from the ceiling of the gym, the lights turned low, and one hundred couples dancing in each other's arms, the band worked its magic. Grayson Babcock, with the mellowest and sweetest sound ever heard on a saxophone, took the lead on "Little White Lies." In the spotlight, I stood up and played my rendition of "Stardust." The repertoire continued with "Five Foot Two, Eyes of Blue," "I'm in the Mood for Love," and "Pennies from Heaven." As the Harvest Dance came to an end at midnight, the dance band played its closing number, "I'll See You in My Dreams." Afterward, Peggy and I went out into the starry night.

My days in the Delavan High School marching band were concluded at the end of my senior year with the Memorial Day parade. Following tradition, the marching band led the parade down the main street. Units of the American Legion, veterans of the two World Wars, men wearing uniforms long outgrown and carrying guns over their shoulders, followed us. Local riders on nervous horses added glamour and excitement. The parade ended on the hill at the Spring Grove Cemetery, where the band and townspeople gathered around the memorial monument to Delavan's war dead. A small man, assigned the task each year, climbed unsteadily up the monument and placed a wreath over the top. The lead trumpet player discreetly withdrew from the band and placed himself behind the hill to play a muted version of "Taps." Then the band broke ranks, and we walked back to the school to change out of our uniforms. With the other graduating seniors, I said my goodbyes and departed, wondering what was to come next.

The announcement came over the radio in the late afternoon of a cold December Sunday in 1941. My father and mother were sitting in the living room with their feet propped close to the hot-air register. Ralph and I were sitting on the sofa, our work clothes already on, waiting to start the evening chores. The program was interrupted: Pearl Harbor had been bombed. A new era was beginning.

All my years of growing up had been years of farming. Life on the farm meant work for everyone. School and play and other adventures took place only after work was done. In the 1940s, the very nature of farming was changing. By the time of my high school graduation, a new form of agriculture had developed. The family farm would never be the same.

Our family, like the families around us, was experiencing the last days of a passing way of life. Electricity had arrived in the mid-1930s. The windmill that had once pumped water from the well had been dismantled. The Delco light plant with its liquid-filled batteries in the basement of the house was used only when the electrical power failed because of an ice storm. Milking machines that allowed a larger number of cows to be milked faster than by hand were installed in the barn. A new model Oliver tractor replaced the old one, and a combine replaced the grain binder and the threshing machine. The tongue on the horse-drawn mower was sawed off and replaced with a new hitch to accommodate the tractor.

But despite these changes, our family seemed in many ways to belong to a former world. We were still small-time farmers, country people in comparison to towns-people. My feelings became mixed: I did not want to grow away from my parents, but at the same time, I wanted to become modern. I could not separate my attitude toward the farm from the one I felt toward my parents.

In August 1945, the war with Japan ended. An atomic bomb killed two hundred thousand people on the other side of the world. The people of Walworth County celebrated victory in the streets of Elkhorn. After finishing the chores and the milking by six in the evening, the earliest time ever in our farming history, we all dressed and drove to Elkhorn. We had to park on the outskirts of town because so many people had arrived to celebrate. Bud Count, who had taken us swimming often during the war years, was at the drums, leading his band for the dancing in the streets. Shortly before midnight, we made our way to the car and home again. In later years, I could not remember if I felt anticipation of a new world or relief in the passing of the old one, but I do remember sensing that something in the lives of our family and in our world would never again be the same.

The daily farm work, always tied closely to the weather and to the passage of the seasons, continued unabated. Winter was a time for allowing the land to slumber under the cover of snow. There were the daily chores of milking the cows and caring for and feeding the farm animals. During the coldest part of winter, as icicles grew longer each day along the eaves of the barn, farm animals went outside only in the warmth of a sunny day.

Of all the winter chores, the morning milking was the most trying. We rose early on the cold mornings to milk the cows. Putting on long underwear and overalls, we left the house and walked in the darkness through snowdrifts to the barn. The cows would get up from their stalls, their breath filling the air. Cats, lazy after the night's sleep, left their beds under the straw to welcome us. The great Holstein bull in the heavily barred stall at the end of the barn bellowed a morning greeting. Ralph and I strapped the milking machines to the first two cows, placed the cold milk cups on their four teats, turned on the valve above the stanchion, and the milking began for another morning.

The small black radio was tuned to WLS, bringing news and music from Chicago and breaking the sounds of the animals and the milking machines. On the mornings when the electricity had gone out because of a storm, we milked the cows using pressure produced by the gasoline-powered engine. If the engine would not start, we were forced to milk the entire herd by hand. We would sit on wooden stools with our heads against the cows' bodies to do the hand milking.

An April breeze signaled a warming of the land. A heavy snowfall might still come well into May, but as the sun grew brighter and as geese were seen flying north in formation, we knew that winter was ending. This was the time when farmers could enjoy the pleasure of going to town every day. We ordered baby chickens at the hatchery, purchased seed corn and grain at the mill, and took plowshares to the blacksmith. I liked to accompany my father to the blacksmith's shop, where we would stand in the darkened room and watch fire and sparks fly from the forge as the blacksmith pounded a hard new edge into red-hot shares.

With spring came the time for the farm animals to give birth. By the end of March, my father would make nightly trips to the pig house. When birth was certain to take place, he would spend the entire night watching over the sows. Without tending, the old sows might roll over onto the new litter, crushing some of the young. The lambs were born without trouble, their mothers sometimes giving birth in the snow. We always felt joy in the lambing of twins. Newborn calves received special attention because of their size and their economic importance to the farm. The veterinarian, Dr. Roland Anderson, made trips to the farm in advance of their births to detect potential problems. If he examined a cow and discovered that the calf's hooves pointed in the wrong direction, he could expect a call eventually at his home in Elkhorn alerting him of the impending birth. To save the life of the calf and often that of the mother, he would be forced to reach into the mother cow and pull out the calf. Many of the calves grew to become milking cows. I took care not to become attached to the calves that were destined to be shipped each fall to the Milwaukee stockyards.

Dr. Anderson had come from Greeley, Colorado, to Walworth County during the Great Depression to start his practice. He was still a man of the West when I knew him. On one of his calls to the farm, he gave me a lariat that he had brought from Colorado. The lariat, a fifteen-foot rope made of the finest pliable sisal with a brass thimble braided into the end, became one of my prized possessions. With great care, Dr. Anderson taught me how to use the lariat, how to twirl it in a wide loop to land the noose around the neck of a calf or cow. Later, I would ride my horse, Sparkplug, to the end of the pasture and rope the cow that had strayed from the herd and bring her back to the barn.

The frogs in the pond down at the old place heralded the arrival of spring. Their croaking and peeping sounded clearly in the evenings as the days grew warmer. The redwinged blackbirds returned to the pond, the males perching on the tops of cattails. They scolded loudly, establishing their territory for the mating and nesting that would soon follow. Mallards returned for nesting along the edge of the pond. Tadpoles began to swim in the shallows, and grasses shot up green all around the pond. The red buds on the silver maples appeared ready to open. There were many wonders of spring in sight, but little time to linger and observe them. Spring brought more work to be done on the farm.

Some of the fields had been plowed during the fall before the snows came. The soft, moist soil in these fields was ready for tilling. The other fields needed to be plowed and disked, and corn stalks and oat stubble had to be turned. At the beginning of preparing the fields, the soil often turned to mud, sticking to the cleats on the huge rear tires of the tractor and dropping off in the driveway as the tractor was driven back from the field. Gradually the land dried in the warm sun, and dust would rise as the fields were worked. Ralph and I would hurry home from school each afternoon to complete the dragging and disking of the fields. Looking over the hood of the green tractor as I pulled the drag from one end of the field to the other, I would feel small against the long horizon. I sang at the top of my lungs as I steered the wheel with the palm of my hand, turning to begin another round.

We planted oats first, pulling the grain drill back and forth over the smooth fields and stopping after each round to refill the oat and fertilizer compartments. We planted corn next, and by the end of May, we watched the green tips of corn emerging from the warm soil planted with seeds only two weeks earlier. With planting completed, we would rest a bit from our labors and wait for the alfalfa, clover, and timothy to mature.

By June the hay was ready for its first cutting. The smell of freshly cut clover would spread over the fields as bees buzzed about gathering pollen. As the hay was cut, it would fall into neat rows behind the mower. Sometimes this ended tragically when the harsh mower cut off the legs of a young rabbit. After leaving the hay in the field for a day or two, we would stack the wagon high with the dried hay. Inevitably, some of it would drop from the hay loader as it was drawn behind the wagon across the fields. After pulling the wagon to the barn, we unloaded the hay into the mow.

Following the haying season came long days of cutting and binding the grain. The tasks for my brother and me included running the grain binder. We would hitch the McCormick-Deering binder, which had once been pulled by two horses, to the Oliver tractor. All day long, with Ralph on the binder adjusting the levers of the cutting blade and releasing the bundles, and with me on the tractor driving, we moved across the oat field. I wore a dust mask, outfitted with a penlight battery, to alleviate my hay fever, caused by the dusty grain. Each year from the time I was seven or eight years old, I complained to my father that I was being worked too hard. As I drove the tractor over rough and hilly fields, I had visions of kids in town playing and loafing while I worked all day long in the hot sun, sneezing my head off.

On a hot summer day, the binder broke down and had to be pulled in for repairs. Sitting on the lawn under the oak tree, I watched my father's attempts to fix the binder. I watched closely as he tried to pry loose a bolt with the new claw hammer that I had recently purchased. Growing more and more irritated at my father's efforts, which I thought inept, and suddenly seeing the hardwood handle of the hammer snap in two, I shouted, "You're the dumbest man I know! I'm so much smarter than you! I don't belong on the farm!" For many years, I remembered my outburst and disrespect as the Hammer Incident, and all these years I have regretted my harsh words and the visible pain I had caused my father.

At the end of the summer, the threshing machine, owned and worked cooperatively with several farm neighbors, was pulled to the field and placed south of the barn. One of my favorite photographs, taken by my mother with the Kodak box camera, shows the threshing machine, powered by the old tractor turning the long, twisted belt, blowing straw into the air and into the growing stack. One man is on the horse-drawn wagon, pitching grain bundles into the hopper of the thresher; another stands atop the enormous machine, tending the threshed oats. A white leghorn hen is in the lower left-hand corner of the picture.

Threshing time depended on the readiness of each farmer's crop of grain. When our grain was threshed, it was the responsibility of my mother to prepare and serve the noon meal to the threshing crew. Several farm wives would come to help her with the large dinner on the two or three days that the crew worked at our farm. My mother would return the help when the crew moved on to another farm. Promptly at noon, the power belt from the tractor was released and the machine would fall silent. The load of grain bundles remaining on the wagon would wait until after the noon hour. The horses were placed in a shady spot and given water, and their feedbags were attached.

The metal-frame washstands, complete with Lava soap and towels, were set up in the back yard. After each thresher washed, immersing his face in the white enamel pan, the water was thrown out and fresh water was poured for the next man. The workers seated themselves on the back porch at the long oak table whose extra leaves had been added, along with additional leaves borrowed from a neighbor, to make a place for everyone. The food would arrive: mashed potatoes, meat, and gravy, followed by hot apple pie and chunks of cheddar cheese for dessert. The smoothness of the mashed potatoes established the quality of the meal. My mother would receive compliments from the well-fed crew, and some men would then wander off to finish the hour with a short nap under the Chinese elms.

The threshing season came just before the Walworth County Fair, and usually threshing was completed before the fair began. To complete the threshing was important because summer's grand finale was the fair, a time to show the livestock and farm products that had been growing during the spring and summer. At the county fair, I would show the pigs I had been caring for all summer. My pigs were not ordinary pigs, but purebred Duroc hogs. By raising purebreds, all with certified registration papers, I avoided selling the pigs for pork at the end of the season. My pigs were either sold as breeding stock or retained another year. At the fair, I would hang out a painted wooden sign to promote my purebred Duroc hogs.

My enterprise—planned from the beginning—had the objective, and ultimately the result, of providing me with the money for a college education. An ordinary fattened pig would sell for about fifty dollars in the winter after nine months of slopping and feeding, but purebreds might bring three hundred and fifty dollars. Moreover, if some of my pigs won prizes at the fair, I would be assured of particularly good sales. When I finally entered college, I did not disclose to my fellow students the source of my financing.

The unstated attraction of the county fair was being able to be away from home for several days. I spent the nights sleeping in a big tent with other 4-H members. During the day, I would roam the fairgrounds unattended and uninhibited. It was a time to greet neighbors on a new territory. My grandfather was always in the Agriculture Building looking at the prize seed corn and vegetables. Farmers sat on and walked around the latest improvements in machinery. Neighbors picnicked on the green, listening to the band. Others viewed horse races and special acts from the grandstand. I would stop often to listen to country music being played in the tent operated by the Janesville radio station WCLO. Food was abundant: Harold Loomer's hamburgers, the Bethel Church's hotdogs, Willard Olson's pronto pups, and peanut-covered ice-cream bars.

In the recesses of the imagination, there is something darkly exotic about the carnival. It was both a source of magic and mystery, as well as a source of fear. Farmers for generations kept their wives and children from the woods beyond the fairgrounds where the carnival workers encamped.

For me, the carnival meant excitement, and I looked forward each year to being caught up in the sounds, vibrant colors, and crowds of the carnival. On the midway, I would see strange-looking men and women beckoning: a woman in tight pants offering darts for popping balloons; and a man with tattooed arms and an opened shirt, holding out three balls to knock down a stack of wooden milk bottles. Walking past a tent with an arcade of machines, I could hear wild noises and see people wandering out with cards dispensed for a penny. Other sights would draw me on: two-headed reptiles, dwarfed men, and bearded ladies; motorcycles roaring inside a rickety-walled inverted dome; revolving wooden animals and dragons painted orange, teal, and red; an octopus-shaped ride ablaze with colored lights reaching up and out into the night sky. And, of course, there was the Ferris wheel. It was always wonderful, especially the time when, after waiting a year to ask her, I finally sat at the top of the Ferris wheel with Kate Seymour.

The county fair did not mean the end of the year's harvesting. The work, however, seemed easy compared to that of the summer, partly because Ralph and I returned to the refuge of school. Our father would spend his days cutting ripe corn, hauling it to the silo-filler, and blowing the chopped corn into the cement silo. After days of fermenting, the chopped corn turned into silage for the winter-feeding of the cows. When the best corn had completely ripened into hard kernels, it was picked by hand, ear by ear, and thrown into the waiting wagon alongside the rows. The wagon was then unloaded, the large golden ears of corn going into permanent cribs and the snow fence cribs constructed to hold the overflow.

After the fall harvest, when winter had set in, my father took care of other aspects of farming, such as equipment maintenance and selling livestock. Taking livestock to market was exciting, for it meant a day away from the farm. On one cold gray winter's day when I was twelve, my father allowed me to stay home from school to help him take a load of pigs to the market in Milwaukee. Like most children who get to go on trips during school days, I looked forward to the trip for many days. Going away with my father on a trip made me feel grown up.

As I helped my father drive the squealing pigs up the ramp into the black Chevy truck, I had to keep telling myself that taking pigs to market was a part of farming. It was difficult to separate my emotional attachment to the animals from the realities of farm life. When the pigs were loaded, and after we waved goodbye to my mother, we turned our attention to the trip.

We drove the sixty miles to the Cudahy stockyards in Milwaukee. At the stockyards, we watched as the pigs were unloaded, weighed, and driven through the wooden gates to their destination. After the pigs were sold, my father and I walked up the stairway to the dining hall where farmers in manure-covered overalls were gathering for lunch. We joined other farmers to sit at a long table for our meal of hot sliced roast beef, mashed potatoes, gravy, with bread and butter on the side.

Later, on the drive back home, I watched from the window as we passed through low-lying farmland, where muskrat houses dotted every pond and marsh, and yellow-branched willow trees lined the banks of the creeks. Looking through the wintry haze, I wondered how other people lived their lives, and I thought of the experiences of this day as ones that I would always remember. Soon we had driven the sixty miles to the farm, just in time to begin the evening chores.

IN THE YEARS between 1940 and 1952, life moved between school, play, and farm work, each activity shaping the others. But my lasting impression was of the profound desire to fill my life with something other than farm work. My father would continuously ask my mother, "Why doesn't that boy want to work?" My most pleasant memories were of things that found a place outside farming, of time left over when farm work was completed or interrupted.

On summer evenings, after the cows had been milked, Ralph and I would jump on our bicycles and head into the sunset. I would be on the Silver King that I had bought used on a farm near Darien and that, with its enormous shock absorber on the front column just above the wheel, made riding easy on even the roughest terrain. We would play out the Lone Ranger and Tonto adventures that we had heard on the radio while doing the chores. We would ride west in the direction of Aunt Lizzie's hay field in the quest of good against the forces of evil. With imaginary silver bullets blazing into the sky, I always knew that my world was bigger than a dairy farm in Wisconsin.

The highlight of the week would come when our father had to go to town for repairs or to purchase supplies. We were disappointed when we had to stay home to complete our chores or continue the planting and harvesting. But our father did not impose this restraint often, and he usually allowed us to go to town with him. He enjoyed the trips to town as much as we did.

Loading the truck always preceded trips to the feed mill in town to have the corn and oats ground into feed for the cows, pigs, sheep, and chickens. Once at the mill in Elkhorn, we would wander around the mill buildings and end up in the office, watching and listening to the kinds of talk that we did not hear at home. Our mother would go to the meat locker to get enough pork and beef from the freezer to last the week. If a hog had recently been butchered and processed, there would be buckets of lard to take home for use in cooking and baking. Stopping for a snack on the way home completed an afternoon in town.

My father was not a talkative man, and frequently he seemed uncomfortable with other people, although his demeanor in no way reflected a preference for avoiding human contact. His awkwardness stemmed, I assume, from the feeling of backwardness that farmers have in the presence of others, especially in town. One bright summer morning, on a trip to town to get something at the hardware store, he greeted a townsman with an unusually verbose display of heartiness. Afterward, as if in explanation or apology, he looked down at me and said, "Always give a friendly hello to people you meet on the street. It shows that you care about others."

On Sundays our family would go to the Delavan Methodist Church. We were sent to Sunday school and were then expected to be present at the eleven o'clock church service, which our parents generally attended. Sitting beside my mother and father, I would wonder what religion meant to them. Neither of my parents sang the hymns, and my mother did not close her eyes when the prayers were given. We were taken faithfully to many of the church activities, but instead of gaining any particular belief, some doctrine that could be believed in with confidence, I privately acquired a habit of wondering about the mysteries of the world. These mysteries absorbed much of my imagination, and to me they became important and necessary, a basis for exploring and appreciating the obscurities of the world.

When I was younger, I often asked my mother to read the Bible to me at bedtime. She would hesitate, as if embarrassed, and then suggest that some other reading might be more appropriate as bedtime reading. Perhaps she thought a terror of the unknown was too much to face in the hour before sleep. Instead, she would bring out *The Rover Boys at School,* a book given to me one Christmas by Uncle Lloyd and Aunt Elsie. It was the story of three brothers left fatherless and sent away to boarding school. The oldest brother, Richard, was "tall and slender, with dark eyes and dark hair. He was a rather quiet boy, one who loved to read and study, although he was not above having a good time now and then, when he felt like breaking loose." The book was filled with the adventures of the brothers away from home, and I never tired of it.

Home was a virtuous territory. This meant the exclusion of things that had to do with the unknown and unexplored sensual regions of life. Anything of this nature was a surprise and meant trouble or embarrassment for everyone concerned. Measures to avoid such embarrassment were usually taken, but there were times when it could not be avoided. Such was the case when several friends and I were rafting down at the pond in the woods and a neighbor girl's bib overalls slipped to one side as she fell off the raft. That brief exposure brought as much embarrassment to me and the other onlookers as it did to the girl.

Even the suggestion of the feminine form was enough to provoke embarrassment. Out in the barn stood Aunt Kate's shapely dress form, and though it was headless and mute, a mere representation of the feminine form, it was capable of arousing strange feelings in the adolescent farm boy. Once in uncharted territory, I asked a neighbor girl to come into the tent that I had constructed beside the house, and the two of us innocently lay together on the canvas cot. My mother discovered us when she pulled away the flap door of the tent to peer in. She gave us cold stares and severe looks for the next two days. By the time I had attained the appropriate age for dating, I had to break down heavy barriers to get enough courage to ask a girl for a date.

In nature and in the landscape, I gained much consolation and hope. The realization that life that was becoming complex and mysterious was a gift brought to me by our neighbor, Burton Hanson. Sometime midway in the 1940s, Burton and his wife, Gladys, had moved from a rented farmhouse near Millard to the Dutcher place, the set of buildings on part of our farm. Next to my parents and relatives, Burton became the most important adult in my life. He was the person who brought me close to nature. Occasionally Burton would take a trip north to the region where he had grown up, near Colby. Returning from one of the trips, he brought me a section of a fallen aspen tree he had sawed off, a section that had been chewed by a beaver. Many years later, the beaver cutting still sits in my bookcase.

Burton took us fishing many evenings after a long day of haying. Along Turtle Creek, we fished for bullheads and sunfish. Catching the fish was only incidental to walking along the bank of the creek and waiting for the sun to set over the marsh. "Man alive," Burton would exclaim whenever someone caught a large fish or when a spectacular sunset lit up the evening sky. "Man alive!"

Burton had skills that were in short supply as the 1940s ended. He was a "handyman" who could repair or build just about anything. Neighbors sometimes questioned his workmanship, but as Burton would tell me: "Anyone can make something, but a good carpenter is one who can repair his mistakes." One summer I worked with Burton, and together we built a beautiful pig house on a farm north of Sharon.

The old farmhouse in which Burton and Gladys lived looked west to the oak knoll at the far edge of the marsh. Before the white settlers moved into southern Wisconsin, the area had been part of an Indian settlement, and arrowheads were found when my father plowed the field next to the wooded hill. There were stories that burial mounds had been dug up at one time and that the disturbers had contracted numerous maladies. Burton would look longingly into the marsh and woods from his house on the hill.

Throughout the summer of 1948, Gladys lay in her bedroom, dying of cancer. Burton installed a buzzer at her bedside so that the bell that he had placed outside her window would alert him if she needed help or comfort. Gone were the days when Gladys and I would play the Sunday prelude at the Millard Baptist Church, Gladys playing the piano and I playing either my trombone or guitar. Gladys's condition worsened slowly, and she died at the end of the summer.

Although a few letters passed between us, I eventually lost contact with Burton. When I was a graduate student at Northwestern University, I visited Burton once in a house in Maywood, a western suburb of Chicago where Burton would live the rest of his life. The last time I saw him was on the day of my father's funeral. Burton had stood with the others for the brief moments at the graveside, and afterward had retreated to the car parked over the hill. Though I had viewed him from a distance through the falling snow, I could see tears in Burton's eyes. We had not tried to speak to each other. There seemed to be no need.

When I returned to live in the Midwest again, in 1983, I regained, or reaffirmed, some of the sentiments of my earlier years. I had grown up with the ideas and feelings acquired from living on a Wisconsin dairy farm. My education in the rural schools of the 1940s continued to provide me with values. In all that I had learned on my travels, my memories of growing up on the farm most surely gave me my identity. As time passed, I had found myself drawn to the land of my birth. More than ever, I viewed myself as a part of nature and the landscape, as an intimate part of the farm. Every blade of grass, every form of life, every force in the land seemed interrelated. I knew finally, in a liberating way, that I would be remembered in the earth.

During one of my visits to the farm shortly before moving back to the Midwest, I drove with my mother the five miles to Delavan to do some laundry at the Laundromat and to talk over a cup of coffee at the Traveler Restaurant. On the way, I asked her many questions about the past. Pointing to the right as we drove the familiar road to town, I asked, "Who used to live on that farm when I was growing up?" My mother replied hesitantly, "I can't remember the name of the family. The farm has changed hands so many times." Then I began to remember the main event associated with the farm: One summer evening in the late 1940s, a farmer new to the area was removing the rack from his truck to convert it into a pigpen. The jack slipped and the rack fell on him, crushing him to death. Every farm that we passed on the way to Delavan took on new meaning. On each place there had been one kind of tragedy or another. I remembered the joys of life—births, marriages, celebrations—but I recalled the tragedies most vividly.

For me, these events were being recalled after a long lapse of time and memory. But for my mother, they were a daily reality. Her daily world was charged with the emotions of a life lived for seventy-five years in the few miles around the farm. For her, forgetting about the past was one of the possible ways of living in the present. To recall constantly the troubles and tragedies of friends and neighbors was the price to pay for living one's life in one place. For years, I had escaped the past and some of the painful ways it can impinge on the present; but as I had learned, no one can escape the past forever.

My flight from the place had been in part an attempt to find a force that would affirm life. In my desire for transcendence, divine or otherwise, I had traveled far beyond the circumscribed existence of rural Wisconsin. But in the process lay the contradiction and the tension; being uprooted, I was now in need of a home.

Back at the farm, I walked the pastures and explored the woods. I went down to the marsh where I had played so often when I was growing up. As I moved among the bogs and through thickets of quaking aspens, under a sky of startling blue, I sensed my oneness with nature and the enveloping universe. Swiftly summer was passing. Before long, the Indian mounds and muskrat houses would be blanketed in snow. Spring would return, and life would renew itself in the woods and marshland. New generations of squirrels and rabbits would stir in the oak groves and along the fencerows; frogs would once more peep and croak late into the night. And through all the passing seasons, the rising sun would cast its light on my father's grave, and on my family's farm.

Coming home was a time of reconciliation. I knew that I would not return with the innocence I had once known as a boy. I was different; the world was different. But, by returning, I had begun to understand the mystery of my own relationship to the land. The place called home was a sacred place. Here, now, I could live fully in the world.

Lodging for the Night

GREAT-GRANDMOTHER BRIDGET, sitting in the kitchen chair placed beside the lilac bush, watched the movement along the far ridge to the south. Two Indian men, two women, and a boy walked toward the oak knoll in the marsh. They had returned once more to say farewell to the place that had been their home. Bridget told my father of the sighting along the ridge, and he in turn told me. Growing up on the farm, I thought about the Indians who had lived on the oak knoll. From the beginning, I wondered if I belonged on this land. In search of my own place, I have been a wanderer all my life.

After more than thirty years of travel, since leaving the farm for college in 1952, I walked along the ridge and found my way through the marsh and climbed up the hill to the tall oaks on the knoll. I, too, had returned once more to the place that had been my home. This time I carried with me my daughter's pet which had died a day earlier. I would bury the dead pet in the sacred ground among the Indian mounds. A red-tailed hawk soared overhead, watching me with my burden as I prepared the burial place. I muttered something about returning the animal to the elements of all creation. A strong fall wind blew over the hill from the west. I shivered from the mystery of the act I was performing as much as from the chill of the wind against my face. I remembered the Indians who had been forced to leave their land, and I feared for my own uprootedness even as I stood on the land of my own beginnings. I hurried out of the oaks, retreating through the marsh and up the ridge to the road, just as dusk descended over the gray day.

A story is told among Orientalists of the pious rabbi of Cracow who traveled far to find a treasure that in a dream lay buried under a distant bridge. Finding the bridge, he was told by the captain of the guard that in his dream the treasure was to be found, not under the bridge, but in Cracow, in the house of the rabbi. Returning home, the rabbi discovered that the treasure had been very near all the time. But this truth could be discovered only by making a journey to a distant region and in an encounter with a stranger.

I, too, had traveled far in search of the treasure—for the meaning of my life—and I, too, had returned. Yet my story had not ended with a certain discovery of the treasure. It still eluded me, the treasure of feeling at home in the world. Could it be that the treasure was not literally in the place, but was buried deep inside me? Another journey of even more uncertain territory lay ahead. If the treasure could not be found, I was doomed to be a wanderer all my life.

Bridget and her husband John fled from Ireland during the potato famine of the 1840s. On my mother's side of the family, the Holloway brothers left North Devon when they no longer could survive on Lord Fortescue's estate. "Come to America," a relative wrote to one of the brothers. "You will be able to make a home here." I am removed from their travel and settlement by only a relatively short time. I grew up on the edges of their frontier; I am a product of their movement over the land. And by the fact of my chosen profession, I am an itinerant moving across the modern landscape.

Were they ever at home, the Potawatomis who lived on the oak knoll, Bridget and John who settled on their land, and my father and mother who made their life on the place? Did they feel at one with the world, a peace that comes from being at home? Or is this a question that only we moderns ask of our lives? We move from one place to another looking for the treasure. Each house we inhabit in the journey holds the promise of a treasure. Yet, in the end, I suspect, the treasure of being at home in the world will be found inside ourselves. The ultimate journey is to a far place that is very near.

"ALL THAT WE ARE is a result of what we have thought." I did not know the words of the Buddha when I was young, but I have lived a life formed as much by thought as by anything else. True, wandering from place to place has been a requirement of my profession. Like the poor scholar in an Irish folktale, I have visited the homes of many along the way. But did I not, out of my early thought, choose to be a wanderer on an uncertain journey? And did I not continue on the journey with the thought that I had to move geographically in order to nurture the soul? Thought has made a life.

Two images, which are seemingly at odds, have commanded my attention since the snows began to fall this winter. They have come from a time long ago. On a road that winds through the ice-age bluffs of southern Wisconsin, I ride with my father and mother and brother to the farming town of Whitewater. Along the way we pass the house of a man who lives the solitary life of a hermit. Through the small window of the tar-papered shack, I see the hermit sitting in front of a kerosene lamp as we pass in the winter's night. In the summer, he is seen only occasionally, working the crop that he has planted beside his house. He is one of the old ones who live alone and who are not understood by those who pass on the highway. The hermit has lived his whole life in this one place.

Around the bend from the hermit's house, we pass the deep pond that fills a kettle in the moraine. In the center of the pond, a figure protrudes from the surface of the water. It is the head of a wooden horse. I have waited with great anticipation to see the head of the horse rise from the water another time. Each time we pass by, I am in awe of the horse in the pond. We are molded by the mysteries that enter our lives.

The head of the horse, emerging from the water, seems to be in such contrast to the hermit, so firmly settled. Only with the passing of many years did I learn that the early Greeks had their own myth about what I was experiencing as a farm boy on a trip through the bluffs. The myth is that of Bellerophon, forced to leave his native land soon after growing to manhood. In a misunderstanding with the King of Argos, he has to move from one country to another. Fleeing across the sea to Lycia, Bellerophon is ordered by the king of that land to find and destroy the Chimera, the invincible monster that lives in rocky caves, ravaging the country all around. Bellerophon, even with all his courage, needs help in the task, and Minerva tells him to ride the snow-white winged horse, Pegasus. On the mighty Pegasus, Bellerophon springs into the air and flies like a shooting star through the clouds to the country where the Chimera lives. He slays the monster and says goodbye to the noble and divine winged horse. Pegasus then rises into the sky and speeds away like lightening. The winged horse is never mounted again by any mortal being. Some say that Jupiter set the winged horse among the stars. As for Bellerophon, a later telling says that because of his eager ambition and the success that led him to think "thoughts too great for man," the gods became angry. The mortal rider of Pegasus wandered alone, avoiding the paths of others until he died.

The hermit may never have seen the pond and the flying horse that emerged from the water around the bend in the road. The hermit had his own thoughts. As in the solitude of Henry David Thoreau in a cabin at the edge of Walden Pond, the hermit knew the importance of being in one place. The hermit had no need to fly into the sky on the winged horse Pegasus; possibly he had an imagination with its own wings, making physical flight unnecessary.

Thoreau writes in his chapter on solitude, "While I enjoy the friendship of the seasons I trust that nothing can make life a burden to me." He then asks the rhetorical question, "What do we want to dwell near to?" The woods are full of companions. "Shall I not have intelligence with the earth? Am I not partly leaves and vegetable mould myself?"

The hermit may have said to himself what Thoreau tells us: "I love to be alone. I never found the companion that was so companionable as solitude." In a paragraph Thoreau gives us the secret of the solitary mind. It is surely what is known today as Zen mind: the mind that is at home with itself because it is aware of its relatedness to everything else. Thoreau tells us from his cabin in the woods, "By a conscious effort of the mind we can stand aloof from actions and their consequences; and all things, good and bad, go by us like a torrent."

"I only know myself as a human entity," Thoreau writes, "the scene, so to speak, of thoughts and affections; and am sensible of a certain doubleness by which I can stand as remote from myself as from another." Each life is, as Thoreau concludes, "a work of the imagination."

The winged horse and the hermit's life are two different ways to gain access to what is beyond the ego-centered self. Imagination allows us to fly outward into a sky where mysteries of the universe dwell. The hermit takes a far journey inward. The hermit, a secular version of the desert fathers of the fourth century, made known to us by Thomas Merton, is lost "in the inner, hidden reality of a self that is transcendent, mysterious, half-known, and lost in Christ." Both the winged horse and the hermit are released from the prison of a confining selfhood; both are on a journey that takes them into the larger world, to a union with the otherness of existence.

We moderns are on our own journey of transcendence. We may seldom speak of coming closer to God, but our journey is the same no matter how we talk. And for many of us today, the journey inward is also a journey across the land. We think that we must move from one place to another to find the meaning of our lives. Will we ever come to a resting place that we can call home?

I look back over my shoulder at the ridge where the Indians returned each season. I, too, continue to come back to the place, to the place of my birth. I long for a sign, an answer perhaps to a question that remains unclear. It has something to do with oneness with all creation, perhaps a form that can come only with death. Maybe I am preparing. As I hurry up the hill, I remind myself again of Rilke's advice to those who seek: "Be patient toward all that is unresolved in your heart. Try to love the questions themselves." And the image of the mortal Bellerophon on the great winged horse Pegasus cautions me to be careful in the questions I ask. Live close to the reality of what is here and now in this place where there is all the wonder of the world.

Rather than be among the scientists, I prefer to dwell with the alchemists, among Loren Eiseley's wizards, "who loved the living world, loved mystery, kept talking birds close to their shoulders, never solved a thing but lived close to where solutions were and did not want them, preferred mystery." The leafless shoots of the lilac bush stand quietly along the foundation of the old house.

THE SLIM CRESCENT of the waning moon rises over the southern ridge. The dark night has come quickly. Leaving the place once again, I drive down the road and out to the main highway which will take me south through small towns and across low-lying prairies. Signs at the crossroads name the families who have farmed the land for generations: Crowley, Streit, Lembcke, Dunham, Melms, and Collins. Half an hour ago, I had left the country road named Quinney.

A fog begins to form, rising from the fields, and moves gently over the highway. Yard lights on the sides of barns cast bluish beams that cut through the gray fog. I slow nearly to a stop when an occasional car approaches from the opposite direction. The lights of roadside taverns brighten the way along the sparsely settled farmland. On the edge of a town, near the state line, the orange neon sign of a dealer beams "OK Used Cars."

I near the town that I currently call home. Turning onto Somonauk Road, a trail once walked by the Indians who lived here, I make my way hesitantly along the few remaining miles. At home, my daughter, an adolescent now, does not ask me the question about what happens to animals when they die. The mystery of life—without answers—has entered her world.

Only a short time ago, I had walked daily the streets and byways of another place. Roger Williams, the pious seeker, had inspired the naming of the city out of his own condition: "And having a sense of God's merciful providence unto me in my distress called the place Providence." I, too, searched with all my attention for the meaning of a life, and I tried to find the source of the melancholy that cast its long shadow over my days.

One might expect that after all the years of thought and intellectual endeavors, I would have gained an understanding of my life and its meaning. But I had reached a point where something more than thought and knowledge were required. As the days and nights turned into years, I had wandered around Providence. Gradually I began to sense a spirit of a former time that hovered over the steeples of the New England churches. Questions not raised in modern science began to emerge. The streets of the city led to a place of the spirit that I had not traveled before. The heart quickened as large white clouds formed in the morning sky over the bay and moved in over the city.

This long seeking is a preparation of the soul. In searching for a place, I have desired to return to the source, to be complete. The fifteenth-century Hindu and Sufi poet Kabir asked, "Do you believe there is some place that will make the soul less thirsty?" I was beginning to find, as I walked the streets in quiet meditation, that home must be found wherever I am, that there is no place where one cannot find wholeness.

The years have passed, and I have left the city; but I cannot say that I have finally found a home. I think that I know the way to travel if a completeness is ever to be found. I no longer ask with such frequency, "What is the meaning of life?" I try to avoid the mortal rider's tempting of the gods with questions that are too great. The meaning is very near at hand, in the mystery of this place where I am now. Yet how am I to live in peace and harmony with the meaning that is there all the time? In this small Midwestern town, where I moved to be near where the Indians once lived, I look out along the horizon and know the difficulty of practicing what is so simple.

The delusion that we are separate from all other things in the universe is hard to break. Perhaps, most likely, the delusion of separateness serves a civilization that has lost the old ways of being an integral part of nature. To be in harmony with the world and all its creatures is not a vision shared by economies and political systems that depend on conflict and dominance for their existence. The American Indian who declared, "The earth and myself are of one mind," and the Eastern sages, who for centuries have shown the compassionate oneness with others, offer a new way that is a very old way. It is so simple a way that we moderns find it difficult in our hearts and minds to accept. We suffer each day in the modern delusion of the self isolated from the rest of the world.

We easily become attached to what does not exist. This sorrow that I feel comes from the memory I hold of the dead things of yesterday. Krishnamurti tells us, "It is yesterday that is sorrow and without cleansing the mind of yesterday there will always be sorrow." Thought itself is sorrow; it is a melancholy of the soul. In a meditative living of each day, I am trying to be aware of the thought that fills the heart with sorrow, and I am trying to let it go. The modern mind is always restless, chattering like a monkey moving from one thing to another, one place to another, desperately trying to remember what has been. I walk among the willows, counting the leaves, and I try to free the mind of the words and memories that imprison me. In emptiness there is a closeness to all that is. There is great beauty beyond all thought and emotion.

A quieting of the mind comes in the awareness of the impermanence of all things, and in ceasing to insist that it is otherwise. A Buddhist master of the Rinzai sect in fourteenth-century Japan warned, "Always bear in mind that life, whose gravest problems are birth and death, is impermanent." Likewise, because there is no entity that can be known and experienced as a permanent self, the desolate image of isolated and unrelated beings is dispelled. A contemporary Buddhist, Stephen Batchelor, tells us, "As this new vision unfolds, our basic anxiety and our sense of meaninglessness are dissolved in the growing awareness of the profound mystery of interrelatedness that permeates all phenomena." I trust that as I begin to arrive at this original home of my relationship to all of nature, I will know who I am, and the treasure may be found.

This morning I begin again, reminiscing about the past and, as I have done for years, fantasizing about the future. I am removing myself from the present moment, as if thinking will aid me in transcending myself. This, I realize, is not truly the way to transcend the self. But old habits, grounded in the ways of the West, do not die easily. The past and future are simply thoughts in the present. "All that we are is the result of what we have thought," *The Dhammapada* again reminds me. The sorrow of the present moment is the memory of a past that no longer exists and a future that will never be until it is the present. Time is thought; and the thought of time is sadness. There is only one question left, and the asking of the question is the answer. The asking is what is happening now and in this place.

My writing at this moment is an unfolding, an experiencing of the impermanence of all things. A Zen master in Providence ends his evening Dharma talk with the parting words, "I hope you only go straight—don't know, get Enlightenment, and save all beings from suffering." In awe, in awareness of this moment, I am at home. The rays of the morning sun bounce against the oval mirror as the red squirrel jumps from limb to limb.

WHAT IS OUR LIFE every day but a spiritual journey to an unknown land? We keep returning to the places of a former time and then moving to new places in our search for a home in the world. In the shelter of a house we seek a place where we can be at peace, where we can experience a place in relation to all other places.

Wizards in this age, we live close to the solutions but do not find them. It may be that we prefer mystery to the answer. More likely, though, we who dwell on this vast land cannot fully live the solutions even when knowing them. With a restless mind that desires more to know than to be, a mind that clings and judges, a mind that fears the void, we will not quiet ourselves. In the sadness of thought, we crave what does not exist. The poor wandering scholar finds shelter in the homes of others.

Still another time I make the trip back to the old place. The wooden horse in the pond, existing now only in my memory, no longer rises from the water in the moraine. Nothing remains of the hermit's shack at the bend of the road. The Potawatomis left long ago. Even their chief, Shabbona, told them, "The red man must leave the land of his youth and find a home in the far west." The wild animals are here no more, having gone toward the setting sun. The lush pastures of the farm are now tangled shrubs and matted grasses.

The problem is that of finding a basis for our lives in the midst of turmoil and suffering. Dogen, thirteenth-century founder of the Japanese Soto sect, wrote a text that is appropriate for our time: "In life there is nothing more than life, in death nothing more than death: we are being born and dying at every moment." Everything, even that which we call the self, is constantly changing from moment to moment. We arrive at the original home when we become aware of the flow of our existence. Beyond that, we accept the mystery, and we are compassionate.

The ridge merges into the horizon. I sit quietly, like Thoreau, being "sensible of a certain doubleness," watching thoughts as they rise and fall and move on to something else. The clouds pass above, and there is little memory of them as new clouds appear in the western sky. The honking of geese overhead, the call of a jay, the breeze rustling dry leaves in the oak tree, all these break down the memories that haunt the restless mind. The wonder of the universe is in this place, and eternity is in this moment. But the mind remembers the passing of time. Walking away again, the poor scholar needs lodging for the night.

A Traveler of Country Roads

Another country song, "On the Road Again," comes over the car radio: "On the road again—goin' places I've never been—seein' things that I may never see again." The road this time stretches out of town over the prairie and through the farm country of northern Illinois. I have decided to spend the summer traveling the roads of DeKalb County. As with all travel, no matter how near or far from home, every moment is a journey of the soul. We spend our lives traveling.

It is time for me to travel across the prairie that surrounds the place I now call home. I am ready once again to be on the road, on a multitude of roads that will lead only to the edges of the county. Travel of such proportion already seems to be of eternal consequence.

In a white car as if on a great steed, I set out from town at noon on each day that is graced by a bright sun. The roads follow the grid pattern of the Midwest land, and I go north, south, east, and west. The stated purpose of my deliberation is to photograph the rural landscape. I have received a small grant from the university that will justify my travel along the roads. I will document the changes that are taking place in this rich agricultural county, a movement from small farms to large farms, the transformations brought about by agribusiness. Still I will see a landscape that is timeless. The transcendent quality of the Midwest, one that survives all human constructions, has to do with the line of the horizon, the way the sky meets the land, the drift of clouds over the fields, the way the sun reflects against the weathered barn. This is the landscape that has brought me back to the Midwest after years of travel in other places.

I watch the sun rise high in the sky. White cumulus clouds float over the prairie as I drive out of town. This is a good day to be photographing. What I am looking for is not yet clear. A discovery of some kind, a way of making some sense of this wandering, this journey. I put on sunglasses and turn on the radio to WQSR, "Northern Illinois' Country Connection," from downtown Sycamore. The land before me is already taking on a heightened look. I place the K2 yellow filter on my 35MM camera. Merle Haggard sings his current country song, "Someday When Things Are Good I'm Goin' to Leave You." This is the country I left years ago and to which I have returned at this time in my life. Maybe I will be able to see anew. There is always the possibility of a rebirth, an awakening.

Of late I have taken to looking at what is very near in any search for the ultimate. Whether I believe in God is no longer the pressing issue. How could I, how could we, ever know enough to believe in God? Belief is not the issue.

How to live daily with a faith in a meaningful existence is the contemporary concern. We are seekers in a world where traditional answers are no longer convincing. We are travelers who aspire to reach beyond the material rationalism of the modern age. The sights and sounds along the country road have a double meaning. They suggest that we are indeed in the world but not of it. Through the camera's viewfinder I have a second look.

I TURN onto one of the many dirt roads in the county. "Travelin' with the rodeo is the only life I know." A large, yellow dog dashes from a farmyard and begins to chase the car. "You're the toughest cowboy in town." Holding the wheel with one hand, I grab the camera and get a shot of the dog in pursuit. "I've always been a travelin' cowboy—now there's no place left to go." The dog gives up the chase. I wish I had tried to settle down. Why this longing of the heart?

The dark blue, cloud-filled sky rises above the great expanse of prairie land. The space beyond the town changes the sensibility of the mind and spirit. At first, one becomes lost in the immensity of the surrounding country. But soon the vastness becomes part of oneself. I, the beholder of the open country, now measure the depth of my own nature. I have become part of the landscape, another creature of nature among many others that share the land, air, and water. In a reshaped space I am, as Gaston Bachelard suggests, elsewhere, dreaming in a world that is immense, both outside and inside. I travel through the country to enter a new realm, to change my nature and to become the nature that I am. This is the landscape of my birth and of my daydreaming when young. I am now in a land near home. As the cultural geographers have reminded us, there is something close to essence, to truth and beauty, in the land of our birth. The land holds a mystery we seek to grasp. The traveler is a gnostic, an artist, and a theologian, delving into the mysteries held by the particular place. We travel in this land to know its secrets, and in so knowing we become part of the landscape.

From the fields, the sweet smell of clover in blossom flows through the open windows of the car. On this late June afternoon, red-winged blackbirds perch on the fences in the lowland. The white clusters of Queen Anne's Lace sway along the roadside in the warm breeze. The telephone poles stretch to the end of the road. I turn left to put the sun at my back, watching the shadows fall against the buildings of another homestead. Merle Haggard's words play softly from the radio: "I'll be one more man that you can say you've had. Someday soon I'll be just one more memory."

THE CAMERA becomes the mind's eye as I travel in the country. With camera in hand, I see what otherwise remains hidden. Mysteries are revealed when I am ready to look, and the camera prompts me to be awake to the unfolding. Drawing from the Buddhist notion of *tathata*, thusness and thatness, Roland Barthes alludes to the nonverbal quality of the photograph. Everything is as it is in the void of the place, in the photograph. "Here it is," a photograph of the landscape, an artifact with its own reality resulting from an experience that has its own immediacy. Travel the same road, and you will also experience the mysteries.

"Lookin' for love in all the wrong places." Turning off County Line Road, I stop and rest in a country cemetery. The names of Irish families are carved on the headstones. In this quiet place, I lie peacefully in the grass. I would be willing to give up much in this life. The farmland stretches out on all sides.

Photographing along these country roads is beginning to have a deeply existential quality. I realize that I am also detached from the landscape. Driving down the roads in my car, I look for something to photograph, and I try to find the hidden meanings as the sun plays its tricks, as my mood changes, as the afternoon passes. More and more frequently, I find myself photographing from the car window, rarely stopping to compose a shot that would take me far from the car. I am relating to the landscape at the same time that I am separating myself from it.

My travel on country roads has become an exploration into the human condition, of my being in the world but not of it. This is both a curse and a salvation. In the Eastern sense, this is the challenge. I am the warrior with a camera traveling a road that stretches into the universe. The stars soon will shine as night falls over the prairie.

DRIVING EAST OF TOWN, I turn off Highway 38 and onto Pritchard Road and travel south. Merle Haggard sings: "I think I'll stay around until I'm sick of home-sweet-home." The driveway of each farm leads back into an ordered world consisting of a house, a barn, some sheds, a granary and corncrib, and a silo. The way is lined by trees planted years ago. I stop the car and photograph the farmyard.

The house, with its surrounding yard and farm buildings, is an intimate and sacred world. This inhabited space is in essence a home. A family lives in the world as it dwells in the house and its immediate surroundings. It has taken years to create a place for souls to dwell. Each farmyard is a unique landscape made first in the selection of the site and then in the building and the planting over the years; it is a habitat for human life. For all those born on the homestead, this will be the most significant place of their lives. Where we are born is a reference for all that follows, the place that we will continue to call home.

My photographing of the landscape, my search for a vision, has turned out to be a symbol of the existential conflict between stability of place and movement through space. In both our social existence and our cosmic condition, we are pulled between staying and leaving, living and dying, hanging on and giving in. To move on, to become, is to leave something behind. In our leaving and dying we wish to be born again. I travel to find a home.

The American landscape, especially that of the Midwest, symbolizes and exemplifies the contrast between place and space. The phenomenologist of the landscape, Yi-Fu Tuan, characterizes the Midwest as a mythical land located at the center of the country, a land that inspires us to move to other places. Growing up in the Midwest, we are torn between staying at home and moving away in order to become something else.

As I travel one of the roads in the northwest corner of the county, Willie Nelson sings, "Pretend I Never Happened": "I'll be leavin' in the mornin' for a place I hope to find; all the places must be better than the ones I leave behind." I stop and take from my wallet a worn, folded piece of paper. From the paper, I read a few lines that I have copied from a T. S. Eliot poem: "We shall not cease from exploration / And the end of all our exploring / Will be to arrive where we started / And know the place for the first time." How can I come to know the place?

In his essays on religion and nothingness, Keiji Nishitani of the Kyoto School of Japanese Zen philosophy, suggests that we wipe away the boundlessness of space when we allow ourselves to live daily, taking things as they come. By a "dropping off of body and mind," we return to a home where all things are dharma-like, as they really are. Such a mode of being is to arrive at the "home-ground," where all things are completely in harmony with what they actually are and ought to be. The home ground is an existence free of care and open to the reality of the world. Travel to this place requires a journey to awareness rather than travel of any geographical distance. Still, it is a journey to a far place.

Willie Nelson sings: "Sometimes it's heaven, and sometimes it's hell, and sometimes I don't even know." I pass another grain elevator, one of the old ones on the line of the Chicago & North Western Railroad. Willie Nelson's song still appeals to me: "Sometimes I take it as far as I can; sometimes I don't even go." The sensibility of the song differs from the idea of the sun rising every morning and the moon rising every night. The country song touches the modern malaise.

We of the West live in an age of lost meaning. We can no longer believe fully in scientific rationalism as the source of all knowledge and human progress. The Enlightenment liberated us from the tradition of one era only to be captured by the materialistic ethic of another. My travel is a journey through the modern era, an attempt to go beyond it and to travel toward a reconstruction. Beneath the ruins of modernism I seek a tradition that allows the esoteric realm to enter our daily lives. Although I continue to have my moments of nostalgia for lost meaning, my purpose is to find a new meaning in our postmodern time.

Beyond the existential nihilism that has resulted from the collapse of scientific rationalism and its materialistic culture is the esoteric tradition that is found especially in Eastern philosophy and religion, but which is also found hidden in the Judeo-Christian tradition of the West. My journey is a romantic one, in that I live between two eras and wish to find meaning in what I am now experiencing. I wish to rise above the conflict and disorder of the modern condition. I wish to be whole again.

The high-voltage power lines cut through the rich fields, carrying nuclear-generated electricity to Chicago, as I listen to "Friend Don't Take Her She's All I Got." Farmhouses and buildings stand abandoned in the fields that are now cash-cropped by corporate landowners. Rows of corn and soybeans run to the edges of old foundations. Large dairy barns are shedding their sidings, and the post-and-beam structures are exposed like the bony skeletons of giant mastodons. Low and sleek metal sheds have replaced the wooden farm buildings. The sun is low in the sky; it is getting too late to take any more photographs. And I am hungry again.

The old landscape, the part of the natural environment that has been shaped by the human presence, is disappearing, and a new one is emerging. The new landscape involves new human relationships and values and an altered relationship to the land. We must not, as J. B. Jackson cautions, dwell on the disappearance of the old to the neglect of present-day realities. This is a transitional landscape that I am photographing, but it is also a landscape with its own unique character.

The country roads that I travel continually cross under or over the state thruway. The land is framed as much by the highways as by the homesteads. The roads and highways that run in all directions increasingly determine the look and spirit of the place. All around there is the juxtaposition of the old and the new. Within this landscape is the emergence of a new order. A new aesthetic is developing that will affect us in ways yet to be determined.

Among the changes we are experiencing is a recognition of the impermanence of all things, including our own lives. Other ages aimed at permanence and immortality. Our time is increasingly one of transience and mortality. Although we might nostalgically prefer living in stone houses with Victorian details, it is the cheaply constructed ranch house with the attached garage that serves our needs. The house that we inhabit may well not outlast us; more likely we will move to several other houses before we no longer have the need to be sheltered in this world. Devotion to a past with a seemingly permanent order is not only inappropriate for contemporary existence, but it is an obstacle to realizing the actuality of our human lives. A Zen poem ends with the line: "Change rules the world forever." My search for a home must be with an awareness of the cosmic fact of impermanence.

NORTH OF DEKALB and east of Sycamore I turn onto Old State Road. Parked with its rear end into the road next to an old milk house is a public school bus that has been converted into a church-school bus. Printed in large letters on the back of the bus is Luke 14:23. As soon as I get home, I look up the passage in the Bible. It is the parable of the great banquet: "Then the master told his servant, 'Go out to the roads and country lanes and make them come in, so that my house may be full.'" There are many, including this traveler, who are on a religious mission.

The seventeenth-century poet Bashō set out near the end of his life on a two-and-a-half-year journey that would take him to the unexplored territory of North Edo. In *Narrow Road to the Deep North,* Bashō describes the journey that involved the casting away of his possessions and attachments, including the casting away of his own self. As Bashō traveled, he became part of the larger world.

A hundred and fifty years later in Denmark, Søren Kierkegaard also wrote an account of a condition of the self, of the typical Western self that refuses to become part of that which is beyond itself. A "sickness unto death," as Kierkegaard called the condition, is the despair we humans experience when we fail to become part of the otherness of the world. We travel in eternity, in all the mystery of the universe, and we travel to lose ourselves to the world.

This thing we call the self, the thing to which we are so attached, can come home only when it gives itself up to the world. A Nishitani notes: "This must be a standpoint where one sees one's own self in all things, in living things, in hills and rivers, towns and hamlets, tiles and stones, and loves all these things 'as oneself.'" We, then, are of the landscape, lost (and found) in the absolute emptiness of space. We have arrived at the home place.

In this immediate moment is an eternity. Time and place have been transcended. Time has no beginning and no end. Confusion, conflict, and fear will inevitably return as we enter the old landscape of ceaseless thought and judgment, of striving and the overwhelming sense of the self. Krishnamurti says that time and thought produce the fear we have of this worldly life. Thought creates fear, and thought is the response to a memory of the past.

The objective is not to control thought and time but to allow the self to be still, to allow it to be lost beyond time and place. It is only with a compassionate mind, one that is free of fear and free of the preconceptions of the past and the expectations of the future, that we can face reality. Travel on country roads leads to such awareness, to an enlightenment and to ultimate reality. With a quiet mind, I will travel a few more miles before the sun sets.

Willie Nelson sings, "I may be makin' a mistake again, but if I lose or win, how will I know?" I turn off the radio. The land spreads around me in all directions. A red-tailed hawk watches from high on a telephone pole. The beauty just is, and there is no need in the moment to know anything else.

After years of traveling on other roads and highways, I have returned to the country roads of the Midwest. In looking for something to photograph in the landscape, I have discovered the importance of watching all things as they rise and pass away, of seeing things as they really are. Experiencing the landscape in silence, in bare attention beyond thought, I have become aware of the absolute world and of the reality beyond words, of all that is immeasurable and mysterious.

The road is a home place in which we may live in eternity. The journey is inward to an unknown place. Home is where I have never been before. Here, now, in this place as I travel, I am at home.

A Winter's Tale

SNOW HAS FALLEN again during the night. The faint light of the morning sun appears in the gray sky and climbs up the far edge of the Golden Years Plaza. In the backyard, starlings gather on the power lines near the transformer. A red squirrel jumps from the oak tree and moves along the top of the ruined lattice fence built long ago by a former tenant. As a reminder, perhaps, of the reality of my existence, I have kept the old fence behind the house I now call home. The wind swirls the snow into drifts, blocking the driveway, and the temperature will not rise above zero today.

Sometime in the days ahead, the sun will be brighter, the snow will begin to melt, and a gentle breeze will warm the land. But now we are in a special season, the season of the long winter. It is a time that always seems devoid of life and renewal. The realization that spring emerges from the quietness of winter does not come easily to us. Until the discovery is made each year, we are in a state of a wintering of the spirit.

Venturing out to face the bitter wind and to gain a footing in the snow will be difficult this morning. But I need the walk after days of confinement at home. I also need a change from this continual reading, a reading that has taken its own course this winter. I have stored up quotations, much as the squirrel in the tree has stored up walnuts to provide sustenance for the season. I have saved quotations such as the one from French philosopher Jacques Monod: "The ancient alliance has been destroyed; man knows at last that he is alone in the universe's indifferent immensity out of which he emerged only by chance." All my reading about quantum physics suggests that each discovery serves only to question further the human ability ever to know the world. Whether in the universe or in the realm of daily existence, our primary relation to the world may well be one of not knowing it. A line from the poet Charles Wright strikes me: "There is so little to say, and so much time to say it in."

The deep tracks of schoolchildren guide me as I make my way through the unplowed street toward town. Crows fly among the branches of the tall silver maples in the watertower park. I am becoming aware in a way that I was not when I first stepped out of the house. I think of Thoreau, the wanderer, who let life flow as he attended to his immediate surroundings. I will let this day be a journey of sorts, a wandering journey.

Remembering the walking meditation exercise of the Zen master Thich Nhat Hanh, I concentrate for the moment on my breath as I inhale and exhale into the cold morning air. As he instructs, I practice lengthening the breath over a period of several minutes, and for several steps I focus entirely on the words "My heart is now at peace." Eventually the mind wanders, and I begin to observe this wandering mind as another event in the morning landscape.

Cars and trucks move slowly along Lincoln Highway, DeKalb's main street. Two blind men, their white aluminum canes darting out in front of them, move along the edge of the highway and find the entrance to Andy's Bar. The front window at Dot's Place is steamed over from the breakfasts that have been fried for truckers since 3:00 A.M. A patrolman, having taken a coffee break, returns to his car. Deciding not to stop at Dot's, I make my way to the university to pick up the accumulated mail. As the limestone gothic tower of Altgeld Hall rises from behind the willows surrounding the lagoon, I delight in the moment.

"We must begin not from metaphysics," the Indian philosopher Ravi Ravindra observes, "but from experience, recognizing ourselves as we are; disintegrated, confused and without will, like chaff driven by the wind." And he instructs that as we begin to wake up, to become mindful, we are no longer at peace, for peace is for those who are either sound asleep or fully awake. "In between is the struggle: a step forward, a relapse, a fall, another moment of seeing—the unknown playing hide-and-seek with the known." In the experience of the present, rather than in explanation, I am seeking a spiritual path that begins where I am at this moment, in this place, at this time, as I wander the streets of this Midwestern town.

I stop this morning at Rog's Tap, by reputation the roughest bar in town. Several men sit at the bar, hovering over their drinks in the darkness of a room warmed by colored lights advertising Budweiser, Schlitz, and Old Style. Sitting at the window, I watch aging passengers as they carry their white-bagged lunches from McDonald's to the Continental Golden Charter bus. The westernbound Chicago & North Western freight train speeds past the old station. On the jukebox, John Conlee sings his song "Nothing Behind You (and Nothing in Sight)":

> Ain't that a hell of a way
> to live out your life
> knowing all your tomorrows
> will be just alike.
> When the worries have stolen
> the dreams from your nights,
> and there's nothing behind you
> and nothing in sight.

The lyrics remind me that there is something I need to look for at the DeKalb Public Library.

THE GRAY MORNING CLOUDS have passed, and now the sun shines brightly against the soft, brown stone of the town's library. During the holidays, my visiting daughter suggested that sometime I read William Wordsworth's narrative poem "The Ruined Cottage." We had been talking about our common condition of being observers of the world as we move from one place to another. The poem, I soon find, is about the wandering poet who meets an aging peddler, a fellow traveler on the road. Upon meeting, the old man says to the poet:

> I see around me here
> Things which you cannot see. We die, my Friend
> Nor we alone, but that which each man loved
> And prized in his peculiar nook of earth
> Dies with him, or is changed, and very soon
> Even of the good is no memorial left.

The peddler then tells "a tale of silent suffering," a story about the woman Margaret who once lived in the cottage and longed for the return of her husband. The peddler describes how Margaret's hope for her husband's return slowly bends and breaks her spirit and finally destroys her life.

What are we to make of life's suffering, the poet wonders, in which such things happen. It is the contemplative mind, the peddler notes, that creates sympathies that "grow with thought." Gone is the husband Robert, who once "dwelt in the poor cottage" and stood "and whistled many a snatch of merry tunes / That had no mirth in them." And gone is Margaret: "She is dead, / And nettles rot and adder sun themselves / Where we have sat together while she nursed / Her infant at her breast." The peddler had observed all this: "A wanderer among the cottages, / I with my pack of winter raiment saw / The hardships of that season." All human artifacts are quietly absorbed into the natural world—while we the wandering observers "thus disturb / The calm of Nature with our restless thoughts." One who wanders from place to place, confronting the mysteries of nature, finds little consolation in creeds or in the thoughts of the inquiring mind.

I wander out of the library, Wordsworth's "dreamer among men, indeed / An idle dreamer," who in thought endures the things that are beheld at home. Yet it is with this thoughtful mind, rather than with the desire for worldly achievement, that the wanderer travels an inner way toward union with the transcendent. The meaning of my worldly existence lies in the experiencing of the holy other in everyday life. The Way, as the Eastern-trained psychotherapist Karlfreid Dürckheim observes, "is that never-ending practice which leads us from the reality that was shaped by our world-ego to the reality that is beyond time and space, and thence towards transparence and new becoming." I wander to end this separation from the wholeness of essential being. I practice ceaselessly to be on the path that leads to wholeness. The wanderer never arrives but is always on the way.

Directly across from the library is the low brick building that is the Ronan-Moore mortuary. I pass the building quickly. It is getting late, and I have not had lunch, and what is the day without at least one stop at Sullivan's? A bumper sticker on a rusted Cutlass Supreme parked at the curb near the library proclaims "One Nuclear Bomb Can Ruin Your Day." Farther down the street, another sticker on a GMC pickup reads "Support Hog Prices — Run Over a Chicken." "Life," Ralph Waldo Emerson writes, "is our dictionary," and books "are for the scholar's idle times." When we "can read God directly," Emerson says, "the hour is too precious to be wasted in other men's transcripts of their readings." Emerson adds: "The office of the scholar is to cheer, to raise, and to guide men by showing them facts amidst appearance. He plies the slow, unhonored, and unpaid task of observation." No hour is lost that is spent on the street — or at Sullivan's tavern.

At the tavern, Shorty, of Hiatt Plumbing and Heating, is already making his afternoon stop at the bar. The four Sullivan brothers are briskly serving the afternoon crowd. A bowl of homemade chili would be just right, with some packaged crackers on the side. Having seen me enter, Albert brings me an Augsburger. I hear a man tell his friend that his spirits would rise ten degrees if it would only warm up a bit.

The old man next to me is drinking his whiskey and beer. He says to me, "I get up late in the morning and walk uptown to get a newspaper. Sometimes I walk over to the lagoon and watch the ducks." He then adds, "We have to have some beauty in life." Finishing his beer and shot of whiskey, he prepares to return to his room to take a nap before watching television until bedtime.

Before leaving the bar, the old man asks, "But what am I to do? And I can't see so good anymore." Knowing that I am moved by his question, he puts on his cap and coat and leaves the bar before I can respond.

The world, certainly my world, remains an unknowable mystery. I do not have a Newtonian model of a world governed by a universal plan that is reducible to scientific laws. If absolute truth exists, it is inaccessible to the human mind. "Whatever we call reality," the Nobel scientist Ilya Prigogine observes, "is revealed to us only through the active construction in which we participate." I am firmly placed inside the truth, and I am its participant. The world is thus open to an understanding from within. A philosopher of science, Herman Weyl, points to the location of our interpretation: "This inner awareness of myself is the basis for the understanding of my fellowmen whom I meet and acknowledge as beings of my own kind, with whom I communicate sometimes so intimately as to share joy and sorrow with them." And this inner awareness is part of everything that is, and everything that is transcendent in the world. From where do we come, then, into this nothingness, this everything? Loren Eiseley proposes an answer: "Out of a dark hat in a closet called Night."

DARKNESS COMES EARLY these winter days. I walk home through the narrow alleys that run north and south behind the numbered streets. Barns and garages and work sheds left from another age line the alleys. Off First Street, I walk into the back doorway of Barb City Manor. Elderly women and a few elderly men are coming out of their rooms into the long hallway. Tables in the cafeteria are being set up for the evening meal. I wonder what wintering is at this time of life.

Wandering this day, as in an entire life, has been a search for home, for a return to wholeness in the world. In the solitude of this day, I have gone into the world in order to leave it, and in leaving it, I have found others on the way. "To leave the 'world,'" Thomas Merton writes, "is to leave oneself first of all and to begin to live for others." The solitary wanderer, instead of being isolated, loses the self to a larger self of others.

The wanderer becomes a part of the universe, even (and especially) in this little town of DeKalb. And in the wandering I enter another place, a transcendent place, as I return to the house I sometimes in the night call home. I know that my true home is not a place bound by walls. It is an inner place beyond this world of self and all its seeking.

IT IS NIGHTTIME, and gusts of snow-filled wind blow against the windows of the old house. I have earned my living this day wandering through the town and visiting its haunts. What is left is the accounting. Thoreau went to his cabin at Walden Pond to write a sacred text about the experiment of living. And the writing of the text, as Stanley Cavell notes in his treatise on *Walden,* was an act of awakening, and thus an act that was also a losing of the self. The writer lives to be lost in the moment of the expression. I write in solitude into the wintering night.

Writing is an emptying of the mind. It is a creating of a silent space that is devoid of facts and fears and confusion. Writing is a release to the silence that is truly the sacred. "When there is silence," Krishnamurti observes, "there is immense, timeless space; then and only then is there a possibility of coming upon that which is the eternal, sacred." Finally, "the mind is absolutely free and silent and one discovers that which is beyond all words, which is timeless." The observer has become the observed, the self is lost, and there is no division between this world and any other. "That," Krishnamurti says, "is what death means—ending, complete ending; and when there is complete ending, something new is born."

Ultimately we are opened to a space that transcends all thoughts and words. The truth is beyond any human expression. We have moved beyond time, as Martin Heidegger suggests we might, in a releasement of ourselves from the material world. The eternal is in the present, without beginning or end. Thus Ludwig Wittgenstein observes: "If we take eternity to mean not infinite temporal duration but timelessness, then eternal life belongs to those who live in the present." As I look up from my night of writing, the clock tells me that three hours have passed, and my experiencing of this time has seemed only a moment. In my writing, in my dying, time has stood still. I have been in the present moment; I have experienced eternity.

"And, ere the stars were visible," Wordsworth writes, ending his tale. The wandering poet and the peddler "attained / A rustic inn, our evening resting place." Now I lay me down to sleep, a wintering soul tonight to keep. Another day I have lived and died. In the morning I will awake, born again to winter's new day.

The Loneliest Sound Is the Whistle of a Train

A TRAIN SPEEDS through the night and enters another prairie town. The whistle blows, a scream into the dark night. Townspeople in their beds turn with a shudder. Dreams already underway take another direction. With luck, on a good night, sleep returns. There is hope for another day.

In the morning—this morning of a rising sun in a clear sky—one person in town gets out of bed and goes to the room that is his study. He opens the closet and removes the camera. Film is placed into the magazine and a yellow filter is fitted over the lens. Give the morning some more time. Then walk downtown to begin the day's work. Although he does not yet know it, there will come a time when he will question this life of being a spectator, of being a detached observer in the quest for knowledge. But on this day—a day planned well in advance—he will go to Sullivan's tavern to photograph through the large window the trains as they pass through this prairie town.

I am that person. The one who now lives here after living in many other places. A life of wandering, yes. But that is not the point of this telling. What we have for the time being is this place, a prairie town in the northern hemisphere of the planet earth, located on the spiral arm of a galaxy called the Milky Way, at the end of an era known as the twentieth century. All this is a part of something called the universe. I will tell you more.

Throughout these days, these days of our unease, we make our way downtown. The ultimate questions loom over us. Being and non-being, fullness and emptiness, God and the great abyss. The age—our contemporary existence—might be characterized as the age of Time Being. We are between ages, yet we have a foot in both: the modernism of the past century and the postmodernism of the future. For the present, we have only what is possible, the time being. And, as W. H. Auden has told us, "The Time Being is, in a sense, the most trying Time of all." In the present, we live daily to redeem ourselves from insignificance. Astride the abyss, we are alive.

The look of this place, this town within which I wander, reflects our time. A landscape that is ambiguous, impermanent, and of mixed and multiple sensibilities. As I walk the streets, make my stops, as I wait for the trains to pass through town, I experience the world as film noir. An Edward Hopper landscape of isolated buildings, abandoned storefronts, a highway along the main street, filling stations old and new, the interiors of restaurants and coffee shops, a melancholy in the air, shadows and light.

A vision has been granted unto us. In the ordinary is the strange and the magnificent. This is our time to be lived in wonder and in compassion. Nighthawks by both day and night, we make our investigations. Ethnographers of everyday life at the close of a century, we sense if not a new beginning, at least a world of many possibilities.

And these possibilities come in a remove from the idolatries that continue to surround us. With the novelist Milan Kundera, I hope for "the wisdom of uncertainty," and for the courage to entertain the ambiguity of the human condition. Most religions and ideologies are founded on a desire for a clear distinction between good and evil, on the need to judge and to punish. Might I, as I walk these streets, witness the essential relativity of things human? Might I look squarely at the absence of a Supreme Judge? I might then know what it is to be truly human, to be connected compassionately to one another, and to be an integral part of the world.

Henry David Thoreau — in another time of cultural crisis — decided to live where he could practice the daily discipline "of looking always at what is to be seen." From his cabin on Walden Pond, he lived deliberately and observed closely the wonders of everyday life. Near the beginning of his accounting, in the book *Walden*, he noted the sounds he heard as he sat in the doorway of his cabin. There were the calls of the birds, the baying of dogs, the distant lowing of cows, the rumbling of wagons over bridges, the ringing of bells in the town, and the chanting of whippoorwills and the wailing of owls in the night. But most of his chapter on sounds is devoted to the trains as they pass on the rails at the edge of the pond a hundred rods south of his cabin. Once again, I feel affinity to Thoreau as yet another train passes through this town, only four blocks from my house. The train whistle unites us over the centuries. We hear much as the train passes.

A century's economy and industry, the ways of communication, the sense of time and discipline are conveyed in the whistle of the train. While Thoreau imagined the steaming locomotive as an iron horse, as a great steed snorting smoke from his nostrils and shaking the earth at his feet, I experience something of another age. A great machine, diesel fueled, with a sound more piercing. And no passengers here on these trains, as compared to Thoreau's trains carrying travelers to Boston and returning them to the country west of Concord. My train carries freight only, speeding east to Chicago, and transporting goods back to the west: corn, coal, oil, refrigerated meats, cars and trucks, cement and steel building materials, and the long lines of piggy-backed boxes on flatbed cars.

The whistle of the train penetrates Walden woods, "sounding like the scream of a hawk sailing over some farmer's yard." Here in DeKalb, repeated blasts of the horn shoot into the bedrooms of our homes. Awakened, across a century and a half, we all are made to feel that we are citizens of the world. With Thoreau, my life has "become my amusement" and never ceases to be novel. No need to look elsewhere for the meaning of existence at the end of this twentieth century. It is here as another train passes through town.

THE SNOWS CAME and covered the ground during the holidays. A cold morning, this morning, and the wind is blowing with a chill of thirty below. The temperature will not rise above zero today.

Change, all is change, nothing remains the same. Not long ago, we went to the basement to get relief from the sweltering heat of the afternoon. At night we slept there to get some relief from the noise of the speeding trains loaded with the summer harvest. This morning, bundled in wool, I make a few notes while listening to Beethoven's last symphony, number nine in D minor. I listen, as well, to the songs of Lou Reed and John Cale in memory of Andy Warhol. With a little more sun, later in the morning, I will drive to the lumber yard. On my way, I hope to photograph the tracks along the abandoned passenger station.

Perhaps it is because of the impermanence of all things that we value life so dearly. And in accepting impermanence, we lessen the suffering that comes in holding on to that which cannot be saved. All things decay and change to something else, this body and self included. I live daily in this town with a faith in what cannot be fully known.

The epistemology of our time is in the attention we give to the world of appearance. In the Western world, we dwell in Plato's cave, between the fire and the wall, watching the shadows dance. But always the yearning for a clearer vision of the thing itself. To be enlightened in some manner. The book of *I Corinthians* reads:

> For now we see though a glass darkly:
> but then face to face:
> now I know in part;
> But then shall I know even as also
> I am known.

In the meantime, there is the wonder of our daily existence. W. H. Auden's words speak to us in town this cold, after-the-holiday morning:

> In the meantime
> There are bills to be paid, machines to keep in repair,
> Irregular verbs to learn, the Time Being to redeem
> From insignificance.

Through our imaginations and our daily observations, we give a semblance of order to what we experience. We make order out of chaos.

Everything is simply as it is. All is perfect: the earth turns, the seasons come and go, the tides rise and fall. We may at times, with some enlightenment, sense the emptiness (the fullness and the oneness) of the ultimate and the absolute. Being human—in body, mind, and heart—we must necessarily give our attention to the relative problems of our existence. The moral questions, however relative they may be, are the questions by which we live daily. Yet we live in two worlds, the absolute and the relative. Such is the challenge of being human.

This day on my way home from the tracks I invoke the Sanskrit word *tathata*. An incantation to the ultimate and the absolute. The "suchness" of reality: everything is as it is, beyond the knowing mind. Reality-in-itself. In the darkening afternoon, I entertain beyond human experience the notion that nothing is born and nothing is dying. Birth and death exist only on the relative plane.

At home I read the words of Thich Nhat Hanh on the waves in the water:

> Observing the ocean, we see that the waves are always there being born and being destroyed. A wave seems to have a beginning and an end. But waves are also water. If a wave is capable of seeing itself as water, it transcends all beginnings and all endings. As far as the waves are concerned, there may be birth and death, but as far as the water is concerned, no birth and no death can be found anywhere. Only if the wave realizes that it is water can it be emancipated from birth and death. When you look into the nature of interbeing, when you know that you are that nature of interbeing, you will be free.

What appears to be film noir—small town noir—in my daily human existence is simply emptiness, or *suchness*, in the realm of the absolute. I may die to the day (I *will* die to the day), but in a larger perspective there will be no death.

I know this in moments of awareness, but still there will be the chill in my spine when the train from the west passes through town tonight and sounds its lonely whistle.

I HOPE TO PHOTOGRAPH the moving train as it passes through town. My attempts up to now have come to naught. Three or four freight trains speed through DeKalb every hour, twenty-four hours a day. But when I wait with the camera on the tripod, no trains appear. I am beginning to sense what it was like for Peter Matthiessen climbing the Himalayas hoping to sight the snow leopard. Finally, as in all journeys, it is the search itself that is important.

At home, at the place I now call home, the whistle can be heard again. A nineteenth-century technology — the train and the whistle. A blasting of the whistle once removed cattle from the right-of-way granted the railroads. Today, a century and a half later, the whistle ceases to serve public safety. Accidents at the crossings and suicides along the tracks are recorded each year in town. I have written to the local newspapers protesting the noise of the train and the ineffectiveness of the whistle. In letters to the editor, I have proposed that the tracks bypass town in the same way that the interstate highway diverts car and truck traffic. Letters from fellow citizens, in response to my letters, suggest nostalgia for trains. Anyone bothered by trains, I am told, can leave town. I think that I am learning to live with trains, as I watch and wait and listen.

Earlier this year, a colleague in the history department observed how our minds reside in disciplines with regional, national, international, and sometimes cosmic directions. Yet, we live daily as citizens, as responsible human beings, here in town. Our bodies and emotions are attached to this place, but only portions of our minds dwell here. Much of the time we are not "here" at all. We make our accommodations, our adjustments; and for me, the events of the here and now—in this Midwest town—are the substance of my intellectual work. The local and global become one and the same. Not just this train in this town, but *the* train—as fact and metaphor—in this turn-of-the-century existence.

Is it not, then, essentially a question of being at home? Our human impulse is to feel at home, to be at one with a place, a place that finally may be the whole of the universe. And it is with some sense of home, of belonging to a place, that we humans have, as Stanley Cavell has noted, "the promise and power of leaving it." With home, we have the possibility of leaving home, of distancing ourselves from the familiar, of wandering into a larger world. Thoreau in building a cabin in the woods near Concord was free to travel a whole world. Each day we leave home. As a wanderer, in thought and spirit as well as in space, I leave town each day.

We are firmly within a philosophical tradition, whether of the East or the West. Friedrich Nietzsche, as a European, wrote: "If you would like to see our European morality for once as it looks from a distance, and if one would like to measure it against other moralities, past and future, then one has to proceed as a wanderer who wants to know how high the towers in a town are: he *leaves* the town." And whether the objective is to compare or simply to live, the wanderer leaves home and enters the marketplace—with helping hands. Leaving home, for whatever duration, is an act of discovery, an act of being human in relation to all others.

I know that I will never be fully at home in this town or in this world. We all are ultimately of some other place; we are born to this world, and we leave it. In the meantime, we search for home and, simultaneously, we long to distance ourselves from it. Such is our human condition.

Yesterday, after a snowfall during the night, I set up my camera at Seventh Street to photograph the tracks. Without expectation, without thought or hope, what do you suppose happened? A train from the west roared toward me, and I quickly pushed the shutter release. The camera on the tripod was overturned by the force of the passing train. Recovering the camera in the snow, I may have captured on film the image of the train. Snow blew in the wind as the train sped out of town toward Chicago.

For some time, I have been reading Robert Burton's *The Anatomy of Melancholy,* that seventeenth-century book which continued to be revised until the author's death in 1640. The writing—and the immense reading upon which the writing is based—was Burton's life. Reading and writing were for Burton life itself.

I read *The Anatomy of Melancholy* for the same reasons today that Burton wrote the book three and half centuries ago. To keep busy and to occupy this gift of the human mind. The paradox of such labor, however: In distracting myself from the ultimate meaning of existence, I raise questions that lead me only further into the abyss.

Burton's book may be known best as a vast dissertation on the psychological state known as melancholy. It is certainly that, a book filled with the immense learning of the past, but it is also (if not primarily) a document of one person attempting to master the proliferation of learning available in published form. The invention of the printing press a century and a half before Burton's time made scholarship readily accessible, and made reading an occupation in itself. Melancholy, sometimes a morbid sadness, was a mental state many claimed to suffer in Burton's century.

The melancholy that concerned and afflicted Burton is the mental and psychological condition that comes with the search for knowledge. The more Burton read about melancholy the more he tried to know the meaning of melancholy, the more he experienced melancholy. And is this not our condition today as intellectuals? The more we seek to know, the more we devise methods of investigation, the more depressed in mind and spirit we become.

Yet we continue to seek the Holy Grail of knowledge. I enter the local bookstore to place another order for a book that I have seen reviewed or cited in something I have read. Perhaps one more book will provide me with the answer (the answer to what?), or one more reading will set me on the right course. I enter the bookstore as if entering a temple, a sanctuary, a sacred place. There is ever the hope of salvation, of finding myself in the word. My bookcases at home are filled with books yet to be read. This winter I have built two more bookcases to hold the overflow.

More snow fell during the night. Rather than shovel the driveway, I will stay indoors and read. Turning to insights beyond the Western tradition, I read again the lines of Chuang Tzu:

> If you persist in reasoning
> About what cannot be understood,
> You will be destroyed
> By the very thing you seek.

Keep it simple today. I will not worry, or speculate about, the missing mass in the universe that is reported in the morning newspaper. The earthquake on the other side of the planet is enough for one day. The distant whistle of the train brings me to attention. Loneliness is only a thought. And so is the abyss.

THE ABIDING PASSION for Robert Burton—lasting a lifetime—was melancholy. Mine has been the search for reality. What is real, and how can reality be known? How

Platonic the questions are, in thought and belief. An order is assumed, an order of "forms" (or "ideas") that transcends observation and experience, a higher realm, pre-existent and eternal. We assume that the human mind, in all its reason, can apprehend a world beyond things physical.

Such is the Western belief system: there is a reality beyond our everyday experience, and this reality can be known by the human mind. That there is more to existence than appearance, that there is an essence beyond our own sense experience. A Western religion, the belief in something that is beyond this world, an eternal unknown, sometimes called God. We are mystics, then, in our spiritual and intellectual lives. We hope to see beyond the shadows of the cave.

Yet this mind of ours cannot know of the existence of anything beyond experience. The mind is limited by its own evolutionary capacity. This grand piano of a mind provides the space for the music (our thoughts) to be played. We humans cannot step outside of our existence; we cannot know if there is anything outside of the grand piano. And we do not know if our existence is other than a dream.

It is not for us to know what cannot be known. To seek such knowledge is beyond our capacity as human beings. The simple teaching of Buddhism wisely informs us: "Only don't know." We have the mind to ask questions of reality, existential and ultimate, but we do not have the capacity to answer the questions. Such is our human condition, as

Albert Camus said, a condition of the absurd. Humility, mixed with wonder, makes more sense than the continuous pursuit of trying to know what cannot be known.

We stand before the mystery of existence. Our humanity is in the recognition of our common inability to know for certain. Our fate, and our saving grace, is to be compassionate human beings. Whatever we attempt to know is known in love. Not in manipulation and control, not in the advancement of a separate self, but in the care for one another. This is reality enough.

In the wisdom of the East, the other word for reality is *enlightenment.* A realm neither of knowing nor not knowing. Neither existence nor nonexistence. Dogen, the thirteenth-century founder of Soto Zen, writes: "This realm of reality is also called enlightenment, and it is also called the inconceivable realm. It is also called wisdom and it is also called not being born and not passing away. Thus all phenomena are not other than the realm of reality; hearing of this nonduality and nondifference, do not give rise to doubt." A place where there is nothing on which to dwell. A silent realm of reality, known (and unknown) in moments of enlightenment.

There is no distinction to be made between the experience of this world and transcendent meaning. Appearance, in the fullness (or emptiness) of awareness in the here and now, is all the meaning in the world. With enlightenment, there is nothing that has to be done.

Only with the dropping off of the self is the nature of all things revealed. Because, as Francis Cook, in his book

Sounds of Valley Streams, writes in a commentary on Dogen, "Reality is nothing but that which we encounter in the absence of the craving, fear, sentimentality, prejudice, discrimination, and judgment that originates in the small self." In other words, reality is experienced when the self (the ego-self) is lost. Then we are enlightened and opened to the reality. An enlightenment that is more than mere satisfaction about the nature of reality; an enlightenment that liberates this human being. A freedom to be at one with the world.

Lives, then, are lived spontaneously without the weight of consequences for oneself. "For this reason, compassion is a very simple matter; one forgets the self and does what is needed," Cook writes. We have thus moved from the search for reality—the craving for reality—to the living of a compassionate life. A compassionate life lived simply by acting in accord with awareness of our oneness with all others and with all things—beyond self, beyond the knowing self. The end is compassion, and the elimination of suffering, rather than knowing reality. Without effort, reality is fully experienced.

"So the point is," Alan Watts notes in his book *The Way of Liberation,* "If you want life, do not cling to it, let it go." And in the phraseology of Zen Buddhism, "You cannot achieve this by thinking, you cannot achieve this by not thinking." We watch the trains go by. We watch, we photograph, we listen—this is our practice for the time being.

The last roll of film from my winter of wandering is being developed. Black and white, night and day, the noise and the silence, the freezing and the melting, loneliness and companionship, life and death—each comes with the other. The lesson of ecology, the lesson of no separate self, is that all things are interdependent and that finally all things are one. May I neither dwell nor not dwell on the question of reality again. This I have learned during the passing of another winter.

Nearly two years have passed since I walked the streets and photographed this prairie town in a certain frame of mind and cast of spirit. The trains still speed through town with blasting horns. Physically the town looks about the same, although a few more of the stores on Lincoln Highway have closed and the buildings stand vacant. I am not bothered nearly as much by the sounds of the train. The telling of this tale was a cure of sorts.

This project came to me, out of need, as I intentionally let myself be open to the questions of existence. My position was one of being on the edge, of being vulnerable to the world. Rather than pretending to be an observer who had it all under control, I opened myself to both the wonder and the horror of existing in a vast and ultimately unknowable universe. I was an observer of a place, a reader of the texts of others, a photographer of abstracted black and white images, a sometime participant in one community or another, a philosopher of everyday life, and a householder. Many voices at once, but such is the price and the reward of letting things happen as they may.

Likely I will soon be leaving this town. I have hopes of a new beginning, of removing myself from the old sensibility. The purpose ultimately is to know how to live compassionately. Knowledge as a practical social skill rather than as an intellectual enterprise. The emphasis, still existential, is on action and a life of participation in the world.

The persistent human problem is that of finding a home, is it not? In his book *At Home in the World*, Michael Jackson, while engaged in ethnographic fieldwork in Aboriginal Australia, turns our existential attention to the problem of home. Home is a lived relationship, he argues, rather than an entity or essence. Our craving for objective knowledge is replaced with a desire to know how to live. "Knowledge then becomes a way of carrying us into more fruitful and caring relationships with others, rather than distancing ourselves from others in the name of objectivity." Knowledge is thus a form of worldly immanence, being with others, here and now. Instead of being alienated from the world, we are at home in the world with others.

The train has taken us metaphorically home. The whistle no longer seems to be the loneliest or loudest of calls. We are in the world together.

Once My Father Traveled West to California

MY FATHER would often tell of the trip he took to California when he was a young man. In September of 1924, when he was twenty-four, and after the fall crops had been harvested, he and his good friend Mervin Kittleson traveled west in the Model T Ford to California. They would stay for six months, returning to Wisconsin in time for spring planting. The souvenirs and relics from his trip still rest in the attic of the farmhouse. Only recently did I find, in the old music cabinet on the front porch, the cards and letters he wrote home and the photographs that he took along the way. I now have a story that I can tell about the one great trip of my father's lifetime.

My father had written the cards and letters to his Aunt Kate and his sister Marjorie. They all continued to live in the house that my great-grandparents John and Bridget built after fleeing the famine in Ireland and settling on the few acres in southeastern Wisconsin. My father would live at the old place until he married my mother in 1930 and moved up to the California-style bungalow that he built upon returning from his trip. I would be born in

1934 followed by the birth of my brother two years later. Another life, of farming and raising a family, followed my father's travel to the west. He often told me that someday he would like to move to town.

He had gone through the eight grades at Dunham School before assuming the responsibility of the farm as his father grew older. He also worked some of the time as a weaver at the Delavan knitting mill, and he had a milk route that continued for some years after he married. He owned one of the first Model Ts in Sugar Creek Township. He once had an Indian motorcycle, but gave it up after skidding and falling on the gravel road. Neighbors would tell me of the good times that he had when he was a young man.

On Monday morning of September 16th, my father and Mervin prepared to begin the trip from the driveway of the Kittleson farm. Several years ago, with my mother and my wife, I visited Mervin's sister Alice. In her nineties, she brought out her family album to show us a photograph of my father and Mervin about to begin the trip to California. In the driveway, they stand beside the Model T, luggage strapped to the running board. Mervin has placed his cap on the radiator, and they are posing before the camera. They are dressed in their traveling suits. Alice kindly gave me the photograph.

Leaving the driveway, my father and Mervin drove southwest to Beloit, then down to Rockford and along the Rock River to Dixon, and then to the Lincoln Highway that would take them all the way west. They reached

Clinton, Iowa, that evening, a distance of 120 miles from home. The first lines, in the six months of cards and letters written home, were on a postcard to Aunt Kate:

> Arrived here at Clinton, Iowa at six o'clock. Are spending the night at the tourist camp. Have just gone over the Mississippi River. Had three flat tires, but didn't have to buy any new ones.

Today Lincoln Highway continues to take travelers west. Each day for nearly twenty years I crossed the busy highway to get the morning newspaper. Travel east or west in this country on US 38, 30, or on Interstate 80 and you are likely to be on or alongside Lincoln Highway. You can travel on Lincoln Highway 3,300 miles from Times Square in New York City to Lincoln Park in San Francisco.

A highway to cross the continent was first proposed in 1912. Once the route was decided upon, after great deliberation among promoters of the automobile, portions of the road began to be surfaced. The first seedling mile was completed near DeKalb, Illinois, in the fall of 1914. Until the great popularity of auto touring in the 1920s, travel over the highway was a pioneering experience. My father and Mervin, reaching Lincoln Highway in their Model T on that September day in 1924, were riding the crest of the great tour west. Road maps, guide books, filling stations, tourist camps, and miles of unpaved roads, all these were part of the new life on the road.

Certainly Aunt Kate would be the first person my father would write to on the trip. Kate, his father's older sister, had taken over some of the duties after my father's mother died, when my father was five. My grandfather never married after Hattie's death, telling my father, "I would never find another woman who would be as good to my children as Hattie was." Kate worked as a dressmaker and seamstress in the homes of the rich in Chicago. She had lived for periods of her life in their houses and apartments. She never married. Kate would have been 69 when my father left for California. Years later, on an April night in 1942, my father came up from the house at the old place and told us that Kate was dying. Shortly afterward, the old house was torn down. For the rest of his life, my father lamented the loss of Kate's button box. Lilac bushes from long ago continue to grow around the crumbling foundation.

My father writes to Kate again after two more days on the road. From North Bend, Nebraska, a few miles west of Omaha:

> Camped last night at Council Bluffs, Iowa. Crossed the river into Omaha, Nebraska this morning. Have driven 64 miles this morning. Most all pavement since we got to Omaha. Have had fine weather so far. Iowa roads were real rough and hilly.

On a postcard written the same day he writes to his sister Marjorie, noting that "we seem to be crossing railroad tracks all the time. The trains go past us but don't have time to wait for us."

Marjorie was 29 when my father started on the trip. She would live only 11 more years, dying of a ruptured appendix in 1935. I have a snapshot of her standing in a long dress in back of the house at the old place. A fur stole is draped around her shoulders, over a checkered coat. She is wearing a fine hat. And she is beautiful.

For most of her life, Marjorie worked in the houses of the wealthy families from Chicago that vacationed around Delavan Lake. Many years later, long after her death, my father revealed to me, reluctantly, that she had owned and operated a tavern a few miles southwest of Delavan on Highway 14 during the last years of her life. Wherever I have lived, I have kept a framed photograph of Marjorie on the bookcase.

Over the years I have tried to learn more about Marjorie. I have talked to aging neighbors who knew her. Once I found the house of the man she had dated for some years, a house I had identified in a photograph from her photograph album. The present owners invited me in and guided me through the house. Marjorie's friend, Lloyd Latta, had operated an auto repair shop back of the house. I was told that his sister Ruby had married a doctor and lived in the big house at the far end of the street. I knocked at the door, and there was no answer. Driving back on Highway 14, I passed what once was the tavern Marjorie owned and operated, now converted to a dance and strip establishment.

My inquiries about Marjorie always have been followed by silence, or maybe by a few fading words about not knowing her that well. I suspect that Marjorie was an independent woman in her time, not choosing to be a farm wife, a teacher, or a secretary. She followed her Aunt Kate's fashions of dress. The styles of Chicago's society women — the women Kate served as seamstress and dressmaker — set the standard. And for a woman to own and run a tavern in the 1930s must have raised eyebrows and brought censure. Marjorie was living as not many women dared to live, and likely she paid a price. I know that my father missed Marjorie for the rest of his life.

On the fifth day of travel, after leaving Omaha, my father and Mervin had reached Laramie, Wyoming. It was Saturday night, and my father writes to Marjorie:

> Camped at Cheyenne, Wyoming last night. Ice in front of our car. Cool here all day. Went to the Methodist church this morning and then Mervin drove 53 miles here to Laramie. We had a hamburger sandwich in Cheyenne and they were only half done. Mine made me sick to my stomach. Never was so sick in my life. Was so weak just couldn't sit up. Mervin went to the store and got some oranges for me and my appetite came right back. Am feeling fine now.

The terrain had changed abruptly since leaving Cheyenne. Gone were the gently rolling plains of eastern

Wyoming, and the ascent of the mountains had begun. The highest elevation on Lincoln Highway would be reached at Sherman Summit, an elevation of 8,835 feet above sea level. The continental divide would be crossed midway in the state. My father continued his Laramie letter to Marjorie with a description of the last day and a half of travel:

> All one sees is hills on both sides covered with big boulders ready to roll down any minute. And some pine trees. Quite a lot of snow also. But, fortunately, have had no tire or car trouble in the last three days.

The cost of gasoline has risen from 13.9 cents a gallon to 20 cents with reports of 30 cents a little farther on. He concludes the letter to Marjorie:

> We meet cars from every state on the Lincoln Highway. Only a couple from Wisconsin. Lots of tourists at the tourist camps. About 15 cars here tonight. We use our pillows twenty-four hours each day. Sleep on them at night. Sit on them all day. We intend to get to Salt Lake City in about three days but you won't have time to write us there. And we don't know which trail we will take from there. But in case of sickness or anything like that a telegram would find us at the tourist camp. Had a chance to get a job with a threshing gang. Will close and make our bed. As ever, your brother.

Two days later, across the continental divide at Rock Springs, my father posts a card to Kate:

> We have been traveling through mountains and deserts for the last day and a half. Haven't seen any trees or green grass in that time. Just sand and rocks. Just had fine dinner here for 35 cents.

The trip thus far—1,400 miles—has cost him only $20, expenses being split between the two of them. "Fine weather here. Good thing as the roads are just dirt roads." They reach Green River, Wyoming. My father takes a photograph of the butte at the turn of the road. Sending the photograph home, he writes: "This is the first town we came to with green trees after spending six days on the desert. Sure looks nice. Was named Green River."

Two more cards are sent to Kate before the travelers reach San Francisco. The salt flats and the uninhabited dry desert beyond Salt Lake City have been crossed. In search of better terrain, they decide upon a southern route that will take them down into the middle of Nevada. To Tonopah and Mina and then up to Carson City. My father writes that they have been two days crossing the desert. The roads are awful. "Just one big hollow after another in the road and dry and dusty." He is writing from a bunk house on a ranch forty miles from any town. The next morning, as they are leaving, my father takes a photograph of Mervin eating a pear near the bunkhouse where they stayed all night.

The next night, now in Mina, my father reports that they are still traveling on bad roads in the mountains and desert. "Broke a spring on the car yesterday but got to town all right and bought a new one and put it in ourselves this forenoon. Every little ways we see wild horse or mustangs near the mountains. See quite a lot of turkeys. One flock of about one hundred." They have traveled, by their calculations, 2,117 miles. "Only 460 miles to San Francisco."

Up to Carson City, over the high Sierra Nevada, through the Donner Pass, and the descent to the valley around Sacramento. Then on to Oakland and a ferry ride across the bay to San Francisco. Extreme changes in landscape and climate certainly were encountered. Nothing is reported on these last miles of the trip west. The travelers were relieved and thankful to have successfully made the long trip from Wisconsin to California. They had been on the road for 18 days. And they were excited, I am sure, and filled with anticipation for what the next months in California might hold for them.

From the time of arriving in San Francisco on October 3rd of 1924 to leaving Los Angeles on March 23rd, 1925, my father wrote 19 letters home to Kate and Marjorie. At least these were the letters saved and eventually stored for 70 years in the music cabinet. Letters were written to others. My father mentions letters being sent to his Aunt Mary, to Mary's son Howard, and to his Uncle Bill in South Dakota, and to his father on the farm. These letters, for whatever reason of family history, have not survived.

Two days after arriving in San Francisco my father writes to Kate. The expenses for the trip from Wisconsin to California have been calculated. A total of $52 each, including all auto expenses, eats, groceries, and camp fees. They are now staying in an auto camp, and the fee of 50 cents a night includes the use of the laundry, hot and cold water, and a shower bath.

> A slow rain all day. Jobs seem to be scarce around this city. If we don't find work here we will start for Los Angeles.

In San Francisco, my father is impressed with "lots of nice homes or rather mansions with beautiful flowers and trees." They buy four pounds of grapes for 15 cents, compared to 30 cents a pound paid for grapes in Delavan.

> Was down to the ocean beach the other afternoon and saw some real waves. And there are all kinds of amusement places where one can spend money.

My father closes the first letter from California with concern and advice that will set a pattern in all his letters.

> I left a gallon bottle with some distilled water in it out in the garage. Will you empty it out sometime so it won't freeze and break the bottle? Don't save the distilled water for it won't be any good.

He says that he will check for mail from home at the post office in Los Angeles. "Feeling fine and hope you folks are the same."

Later in the week he writes a letter to Marjorie. "Got to Los Angeles at noon. Reminds me of Chicago. Buildings sixteen to twenty stories high and people galore." They drove through Hollywood on their way into Los Angeles. "Fine homes with pretty flowers and big palm trees. Surely a rich man's city." But nothing grows without irrigation. "Bought a ten quart pail of oranges for 15 cents today." And signs of the old ailment: "Don't know but what my hay fever is coming back again. Have had one continuous sneezing all day and tonight my head is partly filled up. Felt fine until we got 200 miles south of San Francisco." My father would suffer from hay fever and asthma for the rest of his life on the farm.

My father and Mervin continue to look for work in Los Angeles. "They tell us there is plenty of work out on the ranches but can get that kind of work 365 days a year at home." Later in the week, work is found in a restaurant downtown. "Work from 10 A.M. to 6 P.M. Get two meals. My choice of anything in the restaurant." Mervin finds a restaurant job also, with different hours in another part of town. My father tells Marjorie that "we see lots of signs 'Waitress Wanted' but it is hard for a man to get a job unless he wants to go on a ranch and there isn't one out of twenty-five that knows anything about a ranch. Most of them want city jobs. That's the way with us too."

They begin to explore the city.

> Sunday we went to Sunday school at the Broadway Christian Church and stayed for church also. Then we had dinner and went to Pasadena in the afternoon. When we got to the park they were just getting ready to give a concert. So stayed for that. Was very good. Have a bill of it. Will send it so you can see what it was. Got back to Los Angeles at seven o'clock and went to church again at 7:30.

In the same letter to Marjorie, my father asks, "How is Pa coming with the work? Does he still go to the corner with the milk? Suppose the nights are getting chilly now. Are the potatoes dug and how are they?" Then he reports that three cars from Illinois are parked beside theirs in the auto camp. "Saturday night we all got together and had a regular party. One woman from Chicago is surely a twin sister of Sof. Dunbar. Just kept us laughing all the time. Both of us like this city real well. My head fills up some at night."

Three days later he reports in a letter to Kate that he has quit his job at the restaurant. "The Boss and I didn't agree." But there are other things to do. "Good picture shows here for ten cents. Went to one last night. Jackie Coogan in 'Robinson Crusoe.' Was real good." He observes that they "see all kinds of women barbers here. Also women selling newspapers. Anything to make a living." They are hearing from home. "Got the papers Marjorie sent. Find lots of news in them. Seems good to read home news." In a letter from Mrs. Kittleson, they are told that Morris Johnson was showing the silo fillers a new gun he had when it went off and the bullet went through the screen door of the house and just missed his son Arthur and two other men. My father wonders if the cows now are giving much milk, and suggests that if the chickens are fed all the grain, water, and oyster shells they want, they ought to lay. "Weather is just fine. Sleep nights with our car windows open."

By the end of October they have found jobs again. They are working for the power company putting in forms and pouring concrete. The pay is 50 cents an hour, four dollars a day. They are paid even when the cement mixer breaks down and there is nothing else to do but "kill time." They have changed their living arrangements.

> We have gotten tired of sleeping in the car and eating at restaurants so we rented a two room cottage for five dollars a week here at Huntington Park. It has a real bed, tables and chairs, electric lights, water, and a two burner gas stove. Also have use of laundry and shower bath.

They will work with the power company for the rest of their stay in California.

A week into November my father sends Marjorie a letter written on a Sunday night. He and Mervin have just returned from downtown. "Had supper, got a haircut. Rained all day and still raining steady tonight. Hope it stops before morning as we want to go to work." He plans on saving ten dollars a week while the work lasts.

> There is an Irishman working with us by the name of Jack Brett. He is twenty-eight years old. Has been in this country ten years but has the Irish brogue. Keeps us laughing most of the time. Did you folks trade drakes and gander? It would be better to trade gobbler. Ought to keep four hen turkeys. Ole Rasmusson said he would trade ganders. How many ducks did you keep? If the Ford starts hard there is a five gallon can of winter cylinder oil upstairs in the granary. Suppose it keeps Pa pretty busy doing chores now. Hope you are all well.

The next Sunday night he tells Marjorie about their day of going to the Baptist church in the morning and driving to Venice, Ocean Beach, and Santa Monica in the afternoon. "Was a dandy trip." A perfect day with a clear blue sky and a warm sun. "Will never regret this trip as one could never tell you the sights without seeing them with your own eyes. Mackerel from ten to twelve inches long were being sold from a boat for five cents apiece. All cleaned and scaled at that." At night they went to the Broadway Christian Church. My father tells Marjorie that the weather in California in November is like Wisconsin's August weather. "Does Pa keep all the stock in the barn now nights?"

In December they are offered an increase in pay to 95 cents an hour for putting up steel towers. The work will mean climbing on towers 90 to 100 feet in the air. They will take the examination and work on the high towers.

They continue to receive letters and newspapers from home. My father requests a copy of *True Story* magazine. The Ford breaks down after two bearings burn out. "Our Ford did so much pounding everyone took a good look." They climb to the top of a hill high above Long Beach and view hundreds of oil wells that run night and day seven days a week. "No wonder some get rich from the top of that mountain." For breakfast they cook oatmeal, fry potatoes and bacon and eggs, have bread and butter and cookies, coffee and fruit. During the day—pork chops, beef steak, and sometimes veal chops. Since coming to California, Mervin has gained 13 pounds and my father has gained nine pounds, now weighing 178 pounds. They have moved from the rooms at Fruitland Auto Camp and are living in a cottage near Seal Beach. They continue to go to the movies and have been to some vaudeville shows in Los Angeles. "Is Pa cutting any wood these days and what are you burning to keep warm? How is Dick the canary standing the cold weather? Will ring off hoping you folks are all well."

At Christmastime my father receives in the mail a shirt from Marjorie and a necktie from Kate. "Many thanks to both of you for remembering me." From a girlfriend in Delavan he receives a box of six handkerchiefs, three white ones and three with colored edges, initialed. Kate goes to South Dakota to be with her brother Tom, who dies at the end of the month. Christmas day my father and Mervin are invited to dinner at the Fredrickson's. "Had a good time and a dandy turkey dinner with all that goes with it." They play pool and go to church. On December 28th my father reports the highest tide of the year with the water coming up to their cottage door.

The new year arrives and seals come up on the beach near the cottage. My father kids Marjorie that "maybe you would like a seal skin coat. If so I'll catch you a couple. Ha ha." They continue to work from 7:30 in the morning to 4:30 in the afternoon, with a half hour for lunch, and on Saturdays they quit at one o'clock. They have received a box of homemade fudge from a friend of Mervin's. They have gone to a show titled "What Shall I Do," starring Dorothy Mackaill.

My father always shows concern about family and friends and the chores back home. In a January letter to Marjorie he writes:

> Does Pa water the stock in the barn and does he ever use any bedding? That cement floor is awful cold. Bet Buster is a big dog by now. Did you folks bank the house this winter? Think I'll send my shirt back the middle of the week, then if you'll change it for one with a 15-1/2 collar. There will be quite a change on farms around home this spring when people start moving.

ONCE MY FATHER TRAVELED WEST TO CALIFORNIA   127

And my father is beginning to think about buying a suitcase for when he will have to pack and return home. The old one is pretty well shot.

The February days are getting longer. "Sun rises a few minutes earlier and sets later every night. Real foggy." Oil is gushing 100 feet from a well two miles from the cottage. "Some sight." Shows and vaudeville at Long Beach, and "a glass show where a man made everything you could think of out of glass." A fish dinner, "best I have ever eaten, all for 30 cents." My father asks Kate, "What does Pa want to buy another horse for? Has too many now to farm with." He notices all of the auctions and the selling of farms in a copy of the *Delavan Republic* which Kate has sent to him.

The last week of February my father writes to Marjorie to tell her about the trip to Catalina Island on Sunday. From the boat "Avalon" he took pictures, and

> … if they are good will send some home. There were over 500 passengers on the boat. About ten got seasick and fed the fish. Saw a whale come to the top and gush water in the air three times then disappeared. After we reached Catalina Island we took a ride on the glass bottom boat. Just wonderful to see animal and plant life in the ocean. Could look down in the water to the depth of 75 feet seeing the different kinds of fish, clams and weeds. One sea weed that grows to the surface of the water that potash and iodine are made from called Kelp was real interesting.

On Catalina Island, William Wrigley's mansion is seen in the distance high on the side of the mountain. "Mervin and I thought that we have helped him build it by chewing so much of his gum." Then—"each of us bought a souvenir, an abalone shell. Has all the different colors of the rainbow." He will send home a circular of the deluxe excursion.

The letter of March 2nd to Marjorie begins: "Received your letter today and as dad says to come home will work until March 11th." They are planning on going to Riverside to visit a minister who used to live in Millard—"Mrs. Kittleson said to be sure to go there"—and plan to take a week or more to go to San Diego and Tijuana. "So won't get home until about March 25th." The days are hot, in the 80s, and the beaches are covered with bathers. "Store windows are full of spring hats and everybody says 'spring is surely here.'"

The last letter from California—written to Kate—is dated March 9, 1925, Seal Beach, California.

> We went to Los Angeles Saturday afternoon. Went to the depots to find out about train times, fares and so forth. Think that I will come home on the Southern Pacific for anything that I know of now. I will leave Los Angeles Monday, March 23rd at ten o'clock A.M. and get to Chicago at seven o'clock A.M. Thursday March 26th, and will probably get to Delavan on the one o'clock, Thursday March 26th.

While at the depot my father took notice of whether travelers were using bags or suitcases. "There were ten suitcases to every one bag being used. Suppose its because most of the people were traveling a long ways and had lots of clothes that a traveling bag wouldn't hold." He buys a suitcase: "I bought a black genuine cowhide suitcase and it won't be a bit too big for all I have to put in it." The fare home will be about $105.00. Mervin will be taking the train to Spokane, Washington, to visit relatives. "His train doesn't leave until 6:15 P.M. so he will have a few hours to stroll around by himself after I leave."

They go to Riverside, San Diego, and Tijuana in the days before returning home. "Will call for our last mail here at Seal Beach Saturday March 21st." The last letter home ends: "Could plainly see the snow capped mountains from here Sunday morning which are 50 to 60 miles away. According to the papers eight inches of snow fell in the mountains Saturday, but the weather here was just like spring. No snow. Just a little shower of rain. Guess this is all for this time. Floyd."

The spring crops were planted in the spring of 1925. Tilled in the summer, and harvested in the fall. My father would take more photographs with the camera that he used on the trip to California. In Marjorie's album there is a photograph that Marjorie took of my father with his camera, a year after his return from California, and he is photographing her. On the main street in Delavan, stands my father with his camera, Marjorie's shadow before him.

Seasons came and passed, one after the other in their time. My father met my mother at a dance in Delavan on a Saturday night in the fall of 1929. They were married the next year in September. I was born in 1934 on a day in May. My brother Ralph was born two years later. Mervin farmed for the rest of his life a few miles to the north. Occasionally he came to the house to visit my father.

It has been nearly forty years since my father, on a cold and gray November day, walked into the machine shed while making a repair on the tractor, and died. The next morning, I made the flight from New York City to Milwaukee, and drove in a snowstorm with my cousins sixty miles southwest to the farm. In the darkness of evening, my mother stood waiting. My mother lived alone on the farm until she died thirty years after the death of my father.

Shortly before that November day in 1969, my mother and father had visited us in New York. One morning during the visit my father and I walked along the Bowery in lower Manhattan. We passed homeless men sleeping in the doorways of abandoned buildings. For the first time in my life, I saw tears in my father's eyes. The next morning, as we all stood on the observation deck at Kennedy International waiting for the departing flight for the return of my mother and father to the farm, I was caught by surprise when my father took my hand in his, for the first and last time in our lives, and said goodbye. He had told us at the dinner table the night before that his days were nearing an end; a statement that I said could not be true.

The leather suitcase my father carried on his return from California in 1925 remains on a bench in the dusty attic of the farmhouse. In the music cabinet on the porch is the abalone shell he bought as a souvenir on Catalina Island. On the piano is the tattered sheet music of the song that my father used to sing while we did the chores in the barn: "How 'Ya Gonna Keep 'Em Down On the Farm (After They've Seen Paree)?"

In a gray metal box on a shelf above my desk, I have some letters my father wrote to me after I left home. I read the letters when I have the need to hear the sound of his voice. And as he would say in his letters, this is just dandy with me.

My Mother's Diary

My mother had always told me that when she was a young girl she had kept a diary. I never thought much about the fact that she had kept a diary, and I had not given much thought that it might still exist. Only late in her life, and late in mine, did I actually know that the diary existed, and that I would have an interest in seeing it.

One afternoon while visiting my mother in the farmhouse where she continued to live alone thirty years after the death of my father, as we sat at the dining room table, she quite casually said that her childhood diary was in the top drawer of the buffet. I asked right away — with newly aroused curiosity — if I might read it. I asked if I might take it home to read, promising to return it to the top drawer of the buffet the next weekend. "Oh, you won't find anything of interest in it," she said. "Not much happened in those days," she added. She would have let me take the diary home if I had pursued the request, but I did not. "Some other time," she said.

My mother was born Alice Marie Holloway in the spring of 1906. Her mother, Lorena Taylor, named after the song that had been popular since the time of the Civil War, and William V. B. Holloway—always known as Will—lived on a farm just north of Millard in Walworth County. The Holloways and the Taylors had emigrated from rural England during the middle of the previous century. They produced generations of successful farmers in LaGrange and Sugar Creek Townships. My mother would point to the remains of the various homesteads as we took our Sunday afternoon drives late into her life.

My mother was the only child of my grandparents. A fact that I now realize accounts in some ways for the diary that she began keeping at the age of nine. She wrote each day in the diary until she reached the age of fourteen, shortly before her mother died. In the photograph albums I see my mother standing in the snow beside the farmhouse, playing with her pets on the lawn on a summer's day, riding in a cart pulled by her horse Trixy, and standing beside her father or her mother at family gatherings. And now I read the words that she wrote about her young life while growing up on the farm.

The new diary had been given as a gift to my mother from her mother and father. Of reddish brown leather, measuring 4 by 6 inches, the diary covers the year 1916. The next year she was given "A Line A Day" diary that offered a page for each day for the next five years. The printed Prefatory in the five-year diary provides words of advice on writing in the diary. "You have neither the time nor the inclination, possibly, to keep a full diary. Suppose, however, out of the multitude of matters that crowd each day, you jot down in a line or two those most worthy of remembrance. Such a book will be of the greatest value in after years. What a record of events, incidents, joys, sorrows, successes, failures, things accomplished, things attempted. This book is designed for just such a record." My mother made an entry in the diary each day for the next five years.

I removed the diary from the drawer of the buffet shortly after my mother died. Out of great need, I am certain, to remain in touch as long as I could and in any way possible. I had looked forward to another spring of sitting at the dining room table, being together with my mother, talking, and listening to the gentle rustle of the lace curtains. A few words of encouragement and hope would have followed, and then the waves of goodbye as I would drive away again.

ALICE, now at the age of nine, began her diary. The first entry for the first Sunday of January of 1916: "Papa went to church and Mama and I stayed home." School is beginning for the year; it is snowing; and the days are cold: "It was 20 below zero. Alice Jordan froze her face going to school." (Thursday, January 13, 1916)

> Warmer. It snowed some. Mama played with colored dolls and blocks with me. Mama made me two

little cakes and a pumpkin pie. (Saturday, January 15, 1916)

Papa went to church and in the afternoon we went to Grandma's and we had popcorn. It was very cold. (Sunday, January 16, 1916)

Did not go to school. Very windy. Mama and I played school. (Monday, January 17, 1916)

Went to Elkhorn and bought a dish for Mama and a handkerchief for Papa and an eraser, tablet and composition book. Had dinner at the Hotel. (Saturday, January 22, 1916)

Went to school. It rained. We got some things from Sears and Roebuck. I got some slippers and stockings for my doll. They were white. They were so pretty. On the slippers were the prettiest white bows. (Monday, March 6, 1916)

I played out doors. Mama put a hen nest up for me. I did not get any eggs at night. We got some little pigs. One pig had 16 pigs. Two had 10 apiece. (Saturday, March 11, 1916)

Went to school. We sawed wood. I got 1 egg. I got an invitation to Hazel McQuillen's birthday party. Mama got 25 eggs. (Monday, March 20, 1916)

Her words, her voice, her young life. Growing up on the farm north of Millard, attending the South Heart Prairie School, visiting her grandparents, traveling to church and to town, being cared for by her mother and father, playing with her dolls, gathering eggs from the hen's nest, and the gift of a camera. This is the person that I would know as my mother, the one who would give birth to me and nurture me for a lifetime, the mother that I would be with until the very end. I listen now to Allen Ginsberg reading his Kaddish for his mother. We may be as old as the universe, but at the same time "what came is gone forever every time."

I have found a photograph of the house that my mother often visited, and noted regularly in her diary, a photograph taken on the front lawn of her grandmother and grandfather's house in LaGrange, a mile north of the Holloway farm. Her mother Lorena is standing next to her mother Nellie; grandfather Charles is sitting in a chair on the lawn, in front of the house his father built, and Lorena's brother Lloyd is sitting next to his dog. Not long ago I walked through the house with the present owner, and I imagined the many times that my mother had been in those rooms. My mother carefully labeled the photograph on the back, years after the traveling photographer had stopped to record the family on a summer's day.

Photographs were to play an important part in the everyday lives of my mother's family. At the age of nine, my mother was beginning to take her own photographs, after the purchase of the small Kodak camera.

> Hunted eggs all day. I got 2 eggs for myself and 30 for Mama. Played in the mud with Ma's boots on. Papa went to town. I got my Kodak. (Saturday, March 25, 1916)

> Went to school. Papa went to Whitewater. Someone broke the window playing antiover. Papa got some film for my camera. (Tuesday, April 11, 1916)

In a lengthy entry, my mother records her tenth birthday on April 29:

> Had a birthday party. There were 21 here (all girls). Each one brought me a present. Grandma came and helped Mama with supper. I was 10 years old. (Saturday, April 29, 1916)

She lists the presents that she received from each girl, including hair ribbons, handkerchief, vase, bracelet, book, a bag of candy, perfume, and a box of writing paper. The supper is described, as is the birthday cake with pink candles.

My mother kept an album of the photographs that she was taking with her camera. I read the diary entries and then look longingly at the photographs. How many times have I studied the photograph that she took of her mother and father sitting in the Buick in front of the barn, with Lorena in the back seat? Chickens are in the driveway and a horse is peering over the hood of the car.

I took my camera to school. Teacher showed me how to take a picture. Teacher took a picture of me. Jack (my cat) would not hold still so I could not take his picture. We went to Millard and back in the car. I wore my hat to school. (Tuesday, May 4, 1916)

We had a short auto ride. Took Grandma's picture. I had the headache all day. Papa and I went to the woods. I took a picture of Mama and Papa in the car. Papa took a picture of me at night. (Sunday, May 7, 1916)

Did not go to school. I was not sick. I was lazy. Papa painted some of the garage. Jack (is my cat) slept with me in the afternoon. I got up at 4:30 p.m. Papa painted the milk house. (Monday, May 8, 1916)

Spring and summer. The planting of the fields and the garden. Trips in the car to the nearby towns of Palmyra, Whitewater, Elkhorn, and Delavan. A drive to Lake Geneva to watch fireworks on the fourth of July. Excursions with relatives — with both sets of grandparents, Uncle Lloyd, Aunt Lizzie and Uncle Dewey. To the Opera House in Elkhorn to attend a vaudeville show. Trips to the dentist. Cows and pigs are purchased and sold. And school begins again. My mother is given a bicycle and is learning to ride, but "not very fast." On Christmas day, 1916: "It was Christmas and we went up to Grandma's. Stayed all day."

IT IS A SOBERING EXPERIENCE, an experiment in time, to read the entries for any given day, placed on a single page. Such is diary of the "comparative record for five years," that begins with the entries for the years 1917 through part of 1921. My mother would have reviewed the previous years' entries as she recorded the one for the present day. Her life is being viewed in comparison and in contrast from year to year as she writes in the diary, as she is aging from nine to fifteen. Take the second day of each year, for example:

> Slid down hill with Neil and Ella Bogie and Alice Jordan went too. I got my new sled (Tuesday, January 2, 1917)

> Aunt Elsie came down to make my dress and Uncle Lloyd came after her at night. (Wednesday, January 2, 1918)

> Four below zero this morning. The coldest we have had thus far. A little snow on the ground. Miss Shroble froze her finger. (Thursday, January 2, 1919)

> Twenty-two below zero. Roads were not so bad. Mail came. Wind blew and it was very cold. Pa made out census. (Friday, January 2, 1920)

> Pa went over to see Grandma. She was sick with Neuritis. Nice day. (Sunday, January 2, 1921)

MY MOTHER'S DIARY

THE ENDING, and the near ending, of World War I marks the year of 1918. On the home front, the children attending the one-room South Heart Prairie School observed little of the war. Any rationing must have seemed normal, and economic circumstances must have been comfortable enough on the farm. Of course, there were patriotic celebrations to witness, and in the final weeks of the war, the end was far from certain.

> Everyone got out and broke roads. No school. Beautiful day. Snow 4 feet deep in the road. Uncle Lloyd put cattle in the new barn. (Monday, January 14, 1918)

> Everyone moved with sleighs. Lots of ice and water. Went to school. Am knitting squares for Belgium blanket. (Friday, March 1, 1918)

> Went to Lyden to see the soldiers. 3,000 all on horses. (Thursday, May 16, 1918)

> Paper hanger was here. Papered the parlor and sitting room. (Monday, May 20, 1918)

> Had picnic. Passed in all studies with high standings. Will be in 7th grade next year. (Won 2 prizes). (Friday, May 24, 1918)

> Thrashed in the afternoon. Got 860 bushels of barley. (Wednesday, August 21, 1918)

We went to Delavan to the picnic in Tilden's woods. A soldier that had been a prisoner in Germany two years spoke. (Wednesday, August 28, 1918)

Had salt fish for dinner. (Drank water all the afternoon.) Mama and I picked ducks. Feathers all over. (Thursday, October 24, 1918)

Went to school. Telegram came saying Germany had surrendered. We rang the school bell. The church bells rang in the towns. They rang for an hour. Everyone was excited. (Thursday, November 7, 1918)

This report was not so. That the war was over. Went to school. (Friday, November 8, 1918)

Report came that the war was over. (It is so this time.) Got word at 2 o'clock a.m. People celebrated all day. Went to Elkhorn at night. (Monday, November 11, 1918)

Went to school. Went to town. Took my baby bed down. (Tuesday, November 26, 1918)

That diary entry of November 26th — Went to school. Went to town. Took my baby bed down — epitomizes the ending of an era, in southern Wisconsin and in the young life of my mother. Years later, when my mother was in her nineties, she would lament that her baby bed had been lost when the farm was sold.

MY MOTHER'S DIARY

IN THE FALL of 1919 my mother entered the eighth grade at the school in Millard. Her mother and father would buy her a horse, which she named Trixy, to drive the three miles from the farm to school. Trixy would wait in Patchen's barn while my mother attended the eighth grade in Millard.

> Grandma and Grandpa came down to dinner. We had duck and ice cream. Was a little colder at night. I have had a cough all day. (Wednesday, January 1, 1919)
>
> Went to school. At night went to Woodmen banquet. Played games after supper. They danced. Got home about half past twelve. (Wednesday, February 12, 1919)
>
> Was my birthday. Got a pair of silk gloves and silk stockings from Mama and a box of candy from Papa. (Tuesday, April 29, 1919)
>
> Went to Sunday school in the morning. At night went up to Grandma's. Took her for a little ride. (Sunday, June 1, 1919)
>
> Ma and Pa went to Janesville after a pony. Bought Trixy. Ma drove her home. Trixy is 4 years old. (Friday, July 25, 1919)
>
> Papa went to mill. Drove Trixy for the first time alone. (Tuesday, July 29, 1919)

Went to Parker's hog sale at Janesville. I got a new camera. Mama got a new skirt and waist. (Tuesday, August 19, 1919)

Cooler today. School at Millard went better. Drove Trixy. (Tuesday, September 9, 1919)

Went up to Grandma's. Stayed up there all night. (Saturday, September 27, 1919)

Went to school. Grandma died in the morning. Rained. (Tuesday, September 30, 1919)

We went to the funeral. Rev. Clemons preached. Clear. (Friday, October 2, 1919)

Cold. We did not go to church. Grandpa came down to supper. November has been cold with lots of rain. Up to now I have driven to school every day and put Trixy in Patchen's barn. (Monday, November 30, 1919)

The last year my mother kept a diary for a full year was 1920. She would begin high school in Elkhorn in the fall of that year. A year later her mother died at the age of thirty-eight of Bright's disease. My mother stopped writing in her diary shortly before her mother died. I always knew that my mother missed her mother every day for the rest of her life. She kept an oval framed photograph of her mother on the living room table for the rest of her life.

> We and Uncle Lloyd and Aunt Elsie and Grandpa went to Uncle Frank's to dinner. Snowed and drifted the night before. 18 below. We were going sleigh riding at night, but it was too cold. (Thursday, January 1, 1920)
>
> Elkhorn schools closed until after the flu. Ma and Pa's wedding day. (Tuesday, February 3, 1920)
>
> Went to school. Walked home. Papa went to Delavan and brought home a Victrola. (Friday, February 20, 1920)
>
> Easter. Went to church. Snowed a little. Cold at night. Went up to Aunt Elsie's at night. (Sunday, April 4, 1920)
>
> School picnic at Turtle Lake. Got my diploma and standings. Was valedictorian of my class. (Saturday, June 4, 1920)
>
> Rained. Papa went to town with oats. An aeroplane went over. (Thursday, June 17, 1920)
>
> Nice day. Picked gooseberries and currants. I made some currant jam. (Friday, July 9, 1920)

> Fine day. We all went to Racine. Aunt Rachel went with us. In the afternoon went to the shore of Lake Michigan. At night went to a vaudeville. (Saturday, August 7, 1920)

> I began high school at Elkhorn. Nice day. (Monday, September 13, 1920)

> Moved down to Millard. (Wednesday, November 10, 1920)

> Went up to Uncle Lloyd's. Mrs. Uglow and Myrtle and Elva were there. Had a swell dinner. Stayed to supper. Had oysters. (Saturday, December 25, 1920)

UPON GRADUATING from Elkhorn High School, my mother enrolled in the nine-month course in rural education at Whitewater State Normal College. She then taught the eight grades for five years at the Bay Hill School near Williams Bay. Her teaching career ended, as determined by state law, when she married. As I was growing up, I knew that my mother was applying her teaching skills in the education of my brother and me.

On a summer's evening, while attending a dance in Delavan, my mother met Floyd Quinney, the man that she would marry a year later. They courted—going to the movies, picnicking at Whitewater Lake, and watching the waters on Lake Michigan. On the back of a photograph from June of 1930, my mother wrote:

> A happy day we spent at Whitewater Lake. At nite we went to the show at Delavan. The nite I gave Floyd "the answer."

Shortly afterward, she wrote on the back of another photograph:

> Taken in Milwaukee the day after Floyd gave me my engagement ring. Went to Kenosha, Racine and Milwaukee. Had dinner in Kenosha. Called on Kelloggs in Milwaukee and went to a show. A very happy day.

My mother was twenty-four and my father was thirty when they married in September. The informal wedding was held on the lawn of the house in Millard. After a week's honeymoon traveling to Canada, they settled into the house my father had built on the farm. This is the house that she would live in for the rest of her life. A home for seventy years.

AFTER GROWING UP on the farm, and graduating from college and graduate school, I left Wisconsin to explore a world beyond the farm. I would return for visits two or three times a year. My parents continued to farm the land, gradually scaling down the work in the early sixties. My father died in November of 1969, while making a repair on the tractor, and my mother began her life as a widow. She worked as a volunteer at the nursing home in Delavan for thirty years, and made a batch of cookies each week for the patients. And she kept in contact with her grandchildren and great-grandchildren, remembering each birthday, and visiting them on all the special occasions.

Out of my own need to know my mother better, in my adult years, I moved back to the Midwest in 1983. Weekly I would drive north the sixty miles, usually with my family, to see my mother. In later years we helped her attend to her health needs. She once told my wife that she never imagined that she would get that old—into her nineties—and that in fact she still thought of herself as being a young person. Just before her ninety-third birthday, in April of 1999, she passed away just after we arrived to take her to another doctor's appointment. She had waited for us rather than call the ambulance in the night. My mother had feared that she would be taken from the house, and that she would never be able to return home.

I WAS NOT READY, preparing for the funeral, to be told by the pastor that although we mourn, we mourn with the hope of eternal life. The day after the funeral, I went to the basement of my house and found my copy of W. H. Auden's *Collected Poems* and turned to "Twelve Songs," the poem popularized in the movie "Four Weddings and a Funeral." One stanza of the poem conveys utter hopelessness and despair:

> The stars are not wanted now: put out every one;
> Pack up the moon and dismantle the sun;
> Pour away the ocean and sweep up the wood;
> For nothing now can ever come to any good.

Eventually there would be something that could be called hope. But more than anything, I knew the good fortune I had of being my mother's son, and that I would miss her dearly for the rest of my life.

The church was important to my mother's life. Growing up on the farm north of Millard, she and her father and mother attended church regularly. She made certain that her two sons went to the Methodist Church in Delavan as they were growing up. For thirty years, all of her widowed years, she drove to church each Sunday morning, except in stormy weather or when in poor health. Yet outside of the social institution of the church, I never heard my mother speak of religion, nor mention the word "God." Her concern was in doing the right thing. Doing unto others as you would have others do unto you. She did tell me once that I was in her prayers.

I am fortunate to have lived near my mother during my own aging years. A friend with a similar blessing has suggested that we will forever be changed by the loss of our mothers. My friend from my high-school days wrote to me the day after my mother died, offering words of comfort and support. He quoted a statement he had heard from a minister at Easter time many years ago: "To conquer death we merely have to die." Another friend, from afar, whose mother and father died a few months ago, told me that his own life has changed in unanticipated ways since the deaths of his parents. He said that he realizes now that "life is not practice." We are not preparing for anything; life is what we are doing at the moment. "Everything will work out because it is working out." I am certain that my mother would have agreed.

How many times had I almost asked my mother about her understanding of the meaning of life? How many times had I nearly asked her about death? At the last moment I always withheld the question for fear of disturbing her or intimating that I was anticipating her death. All along it was I who feared the question. Likely my mother would have responded with something like "I don't know," or "You ask such impossible questions." We live the best we can while we are here was the philosophy of her life. My mother, at least in the later years, gave me little direct advice on how to live my life, but I knew from the example of her life, from the way she lived, that life's instructions are clear: Be kind, be thoughtful, be helpful whenever you can.

These days I find myself reading the letters and the many notes of thanks that my mother wrote to me. These letters and notes, as well as the diary that she kept faithfully as a young girl, are in a box on the top shelf of my closet. I get them down and read them whenever I want to hear about her good life. The departing words of each letter remind me that my mother is with me always: "As ever, Mom."

I Am Native to This

> But more than we knew, we had our place in a human movement. What this town and its surrounding prairie grew from, and what they grew into, is the record of my tribe. If I am native to anything, I am native to this.
>
> Wallace Stegner, *Wolf Willow*

TALES ARE TOLD to make sense of this wondrous and ever-changing life. The turn of the new century brought a retirement from a life of teaching at the university. At the same time, the chronic illness, lymphocytic leukemia, which had been progressing for a decade, reached a critical stage that required hospitalization, intensive care, and continuous treatment. Moreover, I was about to make a move back to my native Wisconsin. During the year of the new century I often thought of myself as a modern-day Odysseus on a long journey that would end with a return home to my native land.

As the year progressed, my wife and I spent more of our time at the farm. This is the farm that has belonged to my family for generations, the place of my birth and growing up years. As summer came, and as we went to the farm weekly, I photographed the place that I continue to call home. Even with the decaying of buildings and the aging of artifacts found in drawers and trunks, I was transported by the wonders of the present in this much-loved place. With the coming of fall and winter, solace was found, as always, on the farm.

The account that follows is a chronicle, and an abbreviation, of the year of the new century. As the tale ends, we are settling into a new life. I speak here in the present tense—as the life is being lived.

THE THERMOMETER outside the kitchen window of our house in town has hovered around zero the last several days. My health—or the lack of it—has kept me indoors. On Christmas morning, I opened the front door, and with my back to the sun, pointed the binoculars toward a sheet of white paper, and an image of a partial solar eclipse formed before us. We watched as the moon's shadow passed over the face of the sun. For a few moments, the sparkling snow blanketing the front yard turned to blue.

The night before winter solstice—a night with a wind chill of minus forty degrees—a small screech owl fell down the chimney and into the burning fireplace. Immediately it flew out of the flame and into the living room, landing gracefully on the banister of the stairway. We all gazed carefully at one another. After a while, we coaxed the owl toward the doorway, and it flew out the opened door. We wondered later why we had not spent more time with our visitor. We had wanted, I suppose, to see the owl safely returned to the night.

On the morning of the new year we woke up in the bedroom of the farmhouse. We watched the sun rise over the wooded hills and the snow-covered fields. Long icicles were hanging from the roof of the barn. The branches of the trees surrounding the house, covered with an icing during the night, glistened in the morning light. For a good part of the day, driving in all directions, we meandered over the snow-packed roads that finally led south toward our house across the border.

ANOTHER BLAST of arctic air surges across the northern Plains and down to the Wisconsin and Illinois border. Here in our home in DeKalb, west of Chicago, it is too cold to take a morning's walk downtown. Again, my travels must be close to home.

With a change in my antibiotic prescription, I can now make a noontime visit to the Twins Tavern. Tables and booths are filled with lunchtime customers. I seat myself on one of the tall chairs at the bar that runs the length of the room, and I exchange a few words with fellow customers. The sign over the bar sends the familiar greeting: "Beer—So Much More Than A Breakfast Drink." Ornate handles for the dispensing of draft beer line the counter. New Glarus Spotted Cow is the latest addition to the selections. Packages of potato chips and salted nuts are displayed along the edges of the mirror. Antique fishing tackle, bottles of liquor, and knickknacks of all kinds are displayed on the back wall. The news from WGN is on the television set at the end of the bar. Colored neon lights give a warm glow to the room. A good place on a winter's day.

ON THE FIRST DAY of March, my mother used to tell me that on this day in earlier times the country roads would be traveled by wagons piled high with furniture and trunks as tenant farmers and their families moved to the new place. It seemed that the first of March would always be stormy and that the roads would be filled with snow. Today, at the beginning of a week's visit to Florida, we walk the beaches along the Gulf of Mexico. The sun glistens on the water's surface, shore birds run ahead of us, and we gather rocks and shells from the sand.

This month marks the anniversary of my father's birth over a hundred years ago. He died at the age of sixty-nine, the sixty-ninth year of his life. My father never suggested that I continue in his path as a farmer. He knew that I was not fit for the life of hard work, and perhaps he thought that I might pursue the life that he had dreamed of when young.

Later in the month, after supper, I stand on the back porch of the farmhouse looking out the window into the dark night. The yard light on the corner of the barn cuts through the darkness and casts shadows over the driveway and along the sides of the buildings. I know that no matter how much I might try to bring a life back to the farm, the life I once knew here can never be restored. What is gone is gone forever. A lone opossum crawls through the crack of the barn door. During the night, while we are sleeping, a dusting of snow will cover the land. In the morning, I await the results of the lab test and the CT scan. A line from a poem by Charles Wright ends the month: "Buds hold their breath and sit tight."

AMONG PATCHES OF SNOW, bluets are dotting the lawns in town. Clusters of daffodils have started to bloom. A warm wind blows all day long. After yesterday's thunderstorm, green grass is beginning to appear from under winter's musty mats of brown. The golf course at the country club has turned completely green.

My brother and I have met at the farm to make plans for spring planting. We sit around the kitchen table talking to the district conservationist and to the wildlife biologist from the Department of Natural Resources. In a few weeks we will be planting trees and prairie grasses under the Conservation Reserve Program. Soon the old grasses—primarily reed canary—will be burned around the pond at the old place. Eventually the ecosystem around the pond will be restored and will provide a rejuvenated brooding habitat for water birds. Someday—years from now—the black oaks and burr oaks that we are planting will give shelter and sustenance to other life.

A long time ago, I left rural Wisconsin with thoughts and desires for a life in the larger world. Here I am back on the land that once was my home, and from which I sought my escape. And here I am now trying to preserve and protect the land. But happy that I have also had a life elsewhere.

When in Madison last week for what I thought was a routine appointment with my hematologist, I was asked if the removal of my spleen had been mentioned. The problem is that my white blood counts are low again—with neutrophils below 500. I must begin the four infusions of Rituxan. With low counts, there is the danger of infection again, especially the danger of fungal pneumonia. I wonder and worry about the invasion of the aspergillus fungus that comes with the spring winds that blow over these Midwestern fields. After the infusions, I am relieved to learn that my neutrophils have risen to 2500. My daughter and I celebrate with an early dinner at a Turkish restaurant on Monroe Street.

On the high shelf of my closet, I store the boxes of family letters that have accumulated over the last fifty years. Last week in the top drawer of the desk at the farm I found some of the letters that I wrote home in the 1950s. In one letter to my parents, I tell about my first experience of teaching. I had been sent by Kimball Young, whom I was assisting in graduate school, to the Chicago campus of Northwestern University to administer an examination to a sociology class. My assignment was also to deliver a ten-minute lecture—my first lecture ever—to a class I would find seated in a large auditorium. Later that evening, after returning to my room at the Evanston campus, I wrote to my parents that I had made the long walk up to the lecture table. I ended my letter, "The evening is over and I feel that at last there is something I can do." For the next thirty-two years I would do what I found that I could do. And the letters home continued to be written until there was no longer any reason to write.

THE SONG BIRDS are returning to the farm for another season. I have assisted their return and reproduction by nailing bluebird houses to posts and hanging a wren house on the limb of the lilac bush. Upon these boughs this season, birds will sing their songs. Already, from the kitchen window, I watch as twigs are being brought to the nest.

On the floor of the attic of the farmhouse, in a broken cardboard box, I have found a few trinkets and artifacts rescued from the old house when it was torn down in the 1940s. Among the items is the black-glass rosary that belonged to my father's Aunt Kate. A gray clay pipe rests in the bottom of the box, the pipe that I had seen my great-grandmother Bridget holding in an old photograph. My father told me that she brought the pipe with her from Ireland and smoked it regularly. More of the past can be found in the attic when I am of a disposition to look. Soon I will begin to photograph the ruins at the farm, including the buildings that have deteriorated during my own lifetime.

While gathering wild asparagus along the road for last night's supper, I stood motionless and watched a fox run across the tilled land east of the barn. A weasel scurried into the ditch. A marsh harrier, in sleek silhouette, glided over the stubbled field. Thrushes and thrashers were feeding under the brush in the aging orchard. The invading honeysuckle bloomed profusely along the roadside. Chorus frogs sang in the evening from the pond down at the old place. In the morning, after a night of restful sleep in the room in which I was born, I watched goldfinches gathering for thistle seed at the feeder beyond the kitchen window.

We attend the Memorial Day services in Delavan. The war dead are remembered with a parade through town and a service on the hill at Spring Grove Cemetery. Not since 1952, when I played in the high school band for the last time, had I been a part of the procession to the cemetery. After the service of speeches, prayers, musical numbers, and the firing of guns, Solveig and I walked to the graves of my ancestors to check on the progress of the flowers we had planted beside the stones. I will take my doctor's advice and "make hay while the sun shines."

LET SUMMER BEGIN with an early morning welcome. I rise to Dawn's rose-red fingers, as in Homer's classic *Odyssey*. For weeks I have been reading the classic tale, and I envision myself daily on a wine-dark sea as I cross the prairie on my way to the farm. Some mornings I think of myself rising handsome as a god.

Dawn's lovely locks stream though the layers of fog as I stand early in the morning looking over the fields to the hills east of the barn. Later in the morning a crew of archaeologists will arrive to make systematic probes into the oak knoll that rises from the marsh. The objective is to document the occupation of the land around the marsh by the Potawatomis before European settlement. Someday the archaeologists plan to document the settling of the farm by generations of my family. It is my wish that these acres will become a public preserve for others to enjoy and appreciate in the future. Someday we will be numbered among the old ones who once lived on this land.

On another morning we take our folding chairs and sit again behind the barn to watch the rising goddess of morning, and to listen to the early morning sounds. Barn swallows swoop around us. The great blue heron flies gracefully out of the tamaracks at the edge of the marsh. Song birds are awakening in the trees surrounding the house. The Baltimore oriole emerges from its basket-nest in the Chinese elm. We hear pheasants calling and cackling from the far end of the field across the road. The two Sandhill cranes are pulling sprouted corn from the planted rows and are sending deep-throated rattles into the morning air. The crescent moon with bright Venus to its left hangs in the eastern sky above the old and empty corncrib. To our backs, red Mars sinks below the western horizon.

My neutrophils are on the rise as the summer solstice takes place, as the sun reaches its highest point above the earth's equator. The corn has grown at least eight inches during the last week of this month. The sky-blue blossoms of the chicory plant stand tall along the sides of the road. Large clusters of white flowers cover the elderberry bushes. Ripe mulberries are dropping to the ground.

This is the day that we will attempt to remove the dust and dirt from the basement floor. An overture by Aaron Copeland plays on the classical music station. On the front porch, I sit in the rocking chair between the trunks that came generations ago from the old country.

TWO WOODCHUCKS stand upright looking toward the house. I stand among the shadows in the kitchen so that I will not be seen. A young woodchuck peers from the hole in the granary door. The standing adults will resume their four-legged posture and return to the culvert under the driveway.

I am here alone for a day or two to get some idea of what living in the farmhouse was for my parents. They lived in this house from the time of their marriage in 1930, having built the house during the previous year for the life they would create together. Although it has been cleaned and half-heartedly rearranged since my mother died two years ago, the house is pretty much as she made it her home for the thirty years she lived here alone after my father died. I sense in this house a presence other than my own.

I cannot be at the farm long without imagining that I am a character in Chekhov's play "Uncle Vanya." The

Russian estate on which the drama takes place belongs to the old order that is fading. I, too, am of a passing order, and I am not certain of my place in the coming order. Repairs are being made on the house; the land is rented out to pay the taxes; trees and native grasses are being planted on previously tilled land, and some of the fields are returning to their native state. I am a caretaker with little notion of what is to come.

I have found the deeds to the lands that make up the farm. Acres of land have been acquired by generations of my family over the last 130 years. The first deed is for the few acres purchased by my great-grandfather John Quinney in 1868. He and Bridget settled forever into the house by the lilac buses that overlook the marsh and muskrat pond. Beside his name on the deed is his substitute for a signature — a large X.

THE EARLY EGYPTIANS believed that the appearance of Sirius, the Dog Star, rising with the sun added to the solar heat of the day. Warm and humid southerly winds prevail. A year ago this time, I was in a hospital with life in the balance. A year later after treatments and experiments of various kinds, my disease has stabilized, and I am feeling much better. In mysterious ways, I know that I am blessed.

We are beginning to prepare the ground for next year's garden. It will be the first garden we have planted on the farm, except for this year's three tomato bushes, which are struggling beside the sheep shed. Beyond the farm buildings where once cows grazed, a lone deer forages in the field of corn.

We sit at the kitchen table over a late supper, listening to a hard rain falling. All afternoon the sky has been dark, interspersed with sun-laced cumulus clouds. We watched a large yellow butterfly with wings edged in black fly back and forth over the timothy field. Crickets are already jumping in the grass. On the radio, we are listening to a program of blues music being broadcast from Memphis. Jerry Lee Lewis is interviewed ever so briefly, and a recording of his song on the night train to Memphis is played. The lyric is repeated: "Singin' hallelujah all the way." Solveig tells me I am looking the best I have looked all year. Nothing to be blue about tonight. Hallelujah.

Odysseus still has not made his identity known to his wife. Penelope, as night comes, retires to her bedroom to gain some rest. The goddess Athena, daughter of Zeus and patron of human resourcefulness, gives her comfort. As Homer assures us, "Athena sealed her eyes with welcome sleep." And so to bed for welcome sleep at the end of a day of a summer that is fast fading.

A FULL MOON rises above the racetrack and climbs the far end of the grandstand as night falls and the show begins. George Jones, with a fanfare from the Jones Boys, walks onto the stage to the enthusiastic applause and cheers of the crowd. We have secured our seats early, and have waited as the grandstand fills and the time nears for the appearance of the country star. All the years of writing songs, performing, and of living a life are before us as the lights above the stage flash from one color to another, ending in blue for the start of another slow song. The aging singer gracefully, and humorously, acknowledges his advancing years, working his life into the long list of songs for which he is known. As we slowly walk down the steps of the grandstand and leave the fairgrounds, I comment to our friends that we invest our heroes with qualities that we cannot entirely embody in ourselves. The last days of the county fair—coming on Labor Day weekend—always meant that fall was about to begin.

We wake to cool mornings and the yellowing light of fall. I go down the road, along the fence line, to the bottom of the hill, and photograph the goldenrod in bloom. This time of year, when I was growing up and working in the fields, my father would recite the poem beginning "The goldenrod is yellow." And I remember lying in the field nearby, when I was eight or nine, looking into the formations being created by the white clouds, and suddenly seeing clearly the face of George Washington, and knowing then that I had been chosen to do good works in my life. Sixty years later I look into the sky of billowing clouds and simply entertain the mystery of existence.

THE LEGENDARY HARVEST MOON rose as scheduled shortly after sunset. A harvest moon because it is the closest full moon to the autumnal equinox, and because the moon furnished light for farmers before tractors with headlights came to the harvest. All year I have waited to record in my journal a few lines from the poem by John Keats titled "To Autumn." In a letter to a friend, Keats had written, "How beautiful the season is now—How fine the air."

We have spent a day in Madison with a realtor looking for a house that we might buy. We have entertained the prospect of leaving DeKalb and of living in Madison for some time. Today I am checking on the financial possibilities of a move, a move that will place us closer to the farm and, at the same time, in a larger city, and a city that is the state's capitol. Thirty Sandhill cranes circle high above the farm, gathering in a flock for the fall migration to the south. Thirteen wild turkeys cross the road, and walk into the woods that leads down to the marsh.

The Nobel Peace Prize has been awarded to the United Nations and to its Secretary General, Kofi Annan. The Nobel committee noted that it "wishes in its centenary year to proclaim that the only negotiable route to global peace and cooperation goes by way of the United Nations." In the wake of the attacks on the World Trade Center, and the on-going military response being waged by the United States, the recognition of the international organization is important. I await the morning mail for the arrival of the United Nations flag that I have ordered. I have heard recently the quote from Socrates: "I am not a citizen of Athens or Greece, I am a citizen of the world."

THIS LITTLE HOUSEHOLD is on the move. Before the month is over, the contents of our house in DeKalb must be packed, labeled, and ready to transport north to the farm and to Madison. As the month ends, if all goes well, we will be living in a different house in a different place. The mind is scattered, as the belongings of a lifetime are being scattered.

Most hardcover books I will save and pack into boxes for the move north. Paperbacks that age faster than hardcover books, even paperback editions of my own books, I place in the discard pile that is fast growing on the basement floor. Academic books are more likely to go into the discard pile than literary books. I save most biographies and memoirs. Nature books have a good chance of surviving the cut. And there are the books of sentimental value that will be saved, books given to me as gifts by friends and family. And there are the books that have been crucial to me at various points in my life. The discarded books will go to public libraries for their collections or annual fund-raising sales. Each book has played its part in the living of my life. Books discarded are given my blessing as they enter the cardboard box.

The corn has been picked on the farm. The fields are now in stubble. We set the alarm clock for 4:00 in the morning. When it rings, we slip into our clothes and make our way to the far side of the barn where there is darkness away from the yard light. The Leonid meteor shower is just beginning. Meteors, which are actually the pieces of the comet Tempel-Tuttle, flash across the sky. More than the occasional shooting star we sometimes see in the night sky, we see several streaks of light each minute. We lean against the silo as a fresh breeze comes out of the south. Condensation from the night's dew falls from the high eaves of the barn. After half an hour of gazing and delighting, we return to the kitchen for a cup of coffee, and then go to bed for another four hours of sleep. The soundest sleep of the night.

I continue my night reading of V. S. Naipaul's new novel *Half a Life*. The half a life is the life of a great part of the world's population. Whether you are a refugee, a migrant to another land, or someone who has moved from one class or culture to another, or you have moved from one town to another, you are experiencing half a life. In an interview, Naipaul said that he escaped some of his half-life by being a writer. A writer invents a life in the process of imagination and the construction of a narrative. In the writing, one is creating a life.

Cool, windy, scattered showers, and the possibility of snow flurries—the forecast for the day. There is nothing like a move to make you realize how precious is this life, and how precarious our existence. We travel with cartons of breakable treasures from what once was our home to the place that we hope will eventually become familiar. At the moment, we are feeling that we are aliens in this world.

THE LAST MONTH of the year begins in a mist, and there is the promise of sunshine later in the day. A redheaded woodpecker searches for insects on the bark of the Chinese elm next to the farmhouse. We move back and forth between the three places in a camping mode, from a near-empty house in DeKalb, to the farmhouse now packed with boxes, to the house in Madison that is slowly beginning to look like what may be a home.

The front page of the morning newspaper carries a color photograph of refugees in Afghanistan gathered around small tents set in the sand. I clip the photograph from the paper, fold it and place it in my billfold as a reminder of those who travel under circumstances much less fortunate than ours.

Three camels with riders dressed as the Magi lope down the streets of Elkhorn in the annual Christmas parade. Floats, ponies hitched to carts, and marching bands fill the streets for over an hour on this cold, windy, sunny day. Early in the evening, back at the farm, we light a candle and for the first time talk about the uncertain wisdom of our move. Already we are missing the company of friends, particularly remembering the visits to the house during the critical times of my illness. We promise that we will give care to others as care is needed.

As a graduate student in the fifties at the University of Wisconsin, I would walk along State Street, passing the used bookstores, newsstands, men's clothing stores, art supply stores, groceries, and movie theaters. Once on a winter night, I walked in a snowstorm to hear Bob Scobie and his Dixieland Band play into the night. In recent years, Solveig and I have driven to Madison to gather provisions at the farmers' market held on Saturdays around the Capitol Square. The day we were married several years ago, we drove to Madison to spend the weekend.

We awake in the morning at the farm with an inner peace that has been escaping us these last few weeks. The sun streams through the lace curtains in the south window of the farmhouse, making patterns on the living room wall. A prism high in one of the windows sends rainbow colors dancing on the ceiling. I will take a walk along the fence line, and make my way to the stone pile in the far corner of the field to fetch a rock that I can take back with us to our new home in town.

To avoid having to "dodge the bullet," as my doctor puts it, I must have another round of Rituxan infusions after the holidays. In the meantime, the snow has come in the night, and to the farm we must go to photograph the coming of winter. With the temperature well below freezing, the shutter drops slowly. Chickadees, nuthatches, and a red-bellied woodpecker are eating from the suet blocks on the trees. I make a photograph of the ice-filled birdbath.

Back on the island of Ithaca, after his return, Odysseus was gradually recognized by his son, his old dog Argos, and his nurse Eurycleia who identifies him from the scar on his body. Odysseus's wife Penelope welcomes him to the bed, and Odysseus, with his wife in his arms, knows joy: "Joy, as warm as the joy that shipwrecked sailors feel when they catch sight of land." In the morning, Dawn with her rose-red fingers shines upon their happiness.

We are witnesses to a time and a place. This is my time and place. The time is the present. The place is this middle border, a borderland that is home to me. And I am still moving between town and country. But it is to the farm, the farm of the generations of my family, that I always return. This is the place to which I am native.

Photographs

1. Grain Binder and Tractor, with Ralph, Earl, and Floyd Quinney, 1944 (p. x)
2. The Marsh at the Farm, 2000 (p. 40)
3. Sunday School Bus, DeKalb County, 1984 (p. 58)
4. Alley in DeKalb, December 1985 (p. 74)
5. Train Speeding through DeKalb, 1995 (p. 88)
6. Mervin Kittleson and Floyd Quinney, Trip to California, 1924 (p. 108)
7. Alice Holloway and Trixy, 1919 (p. 132)
8. The Farm, 2003 (p. 154)

Bibliography

Auden, W. H. *Collected Poems*. Ed. Edward Mendelson. New York: Vintage, 1991.

Bachelard, Gaston. *The Poetics of Space*. Trans. Maria Jolas. Boston: Beacon Press, 1969.

Barthes, Roland. *Camera Lucida: Reflections on Photography*. Trans. Richard Howard. New York: Hill and Wang, 1981.

Bashō. *The Narrow Road to the Deep North and Other Travel Essays*. Trans. Nobuyuki Yuasa. New York: Penguin, 1966.

Batchelor, Stephen. *Alone with Others: An Existential Approach to Buddhism*. New York: Grove Press, 1983.

Blanchot, Maurice. *The Space of Literature*. Trans. Ann Smock. Lincoln: University of Nebraska Press, 1982.

Burton, Robert. *The Anatomy of Melancholy*. Eighth edition. Philadelphia: J. W. Moore, 1857.

Camus, Albert. *The Myth of Sisyphus and Other Essays*. 1955. Trans. Justin O'Brien. New York: Alfred A. Knopf, 1991.

Cavell, Stanley. *The Senses of Walden*. San Francisco: North Point Press, 1981.

Chaucer, Geoffrey. *The Canterbury Tales*. Trans. Nevill Coghill. Baltimore: Penguin Books, 1962.

Chekhov, Anton. *Five Plays.* Trans. Ronald Hingley. New York: Oxford University Press, 1980.

Cleary, Thomas, Ed. and trans. *Rational Zen: The Mind of Dogen Zenji.* Boston: Shambhala, 1992.

Cleary, Thomas, Ed. and trans. *Zen Essences: The Science of Freedom.* Boston: Shambhala, 1989.

Cook, Francis H. *Sounds of Valley Streams: Enlightenment in Dogen's Zen.* Albany: State University of New York Press, 1989.

Dürckheim, Karlfried. *The Way of Transformation: Daily Life as Spiritual Exercise.* London: George Allen and Unwin, 1971.

Eiseley, Loren, *The Innocent Assassins.* New York: Scribner's, 1973.

Eiseley, Loren, *The Night Country.* New York: Scribner's, 1971.

Eliade, Mircea. *The Sacred and the Profane: The Nature of Religion.* Trans. Willard R. Trask. New York: Harcourt, Brace and World, 1959.

Eliot, T. S. *The Complete Poems and Plays.* London: Faber and Faber, 1969.

Emerson, Ralph Waldo. *The Selected Writings of Ralph Waldo Emerson.* Ed. Brooks Atkinson. New York: Random House, 1968.

Frost, Robert. *Collected Poems, Prose, & Plays.* New York: The Library of America, 1995.

Garland, Hamlin. *Back-Trailers from the Middle Border.* New York: Macmillan, 1928.

Garland, Hamlin. *A Son of the Middle Border.* Lincoln: University of Nebraska Press, 1979.

Goodrich, Lloyd. *Edward Hopper.* New York: Harry N. Abrams, 1983.

Hanh, Thich Nhat. *Being Peace.* Berkeley: Parallax Press, 1987.

Hanh, Thich Nhat. *The Miracle of Mindfulness.* Boston: Beacon Press, 1975.

Hayden, Tom. *Irish on the Inside: In Search of the Soul of Irish America.* New York: Verso, 2001.

Hokanson, Drake. *The Lincoln Highway: Mainstreet Across America.* Iowa City: University of Iowa Press, 1988.

Homer. *Odyssey.* Trans. Robert Fagles. New York: Viking Penguin, 1996.

Jackson, J. B. *The Necessity for Ruins, and Other Topics.* Amherst: University of Massachusetts Press, 1980.

Jackson, Michael. *At Home in the World.* Durham: Duke University Press, 1995.

Kierkegaard, Søren. *The Diary of Søren Kierkegaard.* Ed. Peter P. Rohde. New York: Philosophical Library, 1960.

Krishnamurti. J. *Freedom from the Known.* New York: Harper & Row, 1975.

Krishnamurti, J. *Krishnamurti's Notebook.* New York: Harper & Row, 1976.

Kundera, Milan. *The Art of the Novel.* London: Faber and Faber, 1988.

Lao-Tzu. *Tao Te Ching.* Trans. Stephen Mitchell. New York: Harper & Row, 1988.

Leopold, Aldo. *A Sand County Almanac.* New York: Oxford University Press, 1966.

Liebling, Jerome, et al., *The Dickinsons of Amherst.* Hanover: University Press of New England, 2001.

Maezumi, Hakuyu Taizan. *The Way of Everyday Life.* Los Angeles: Zen Center, 1978.

Matthiessen, Peter. *The Snow Leopard.* New York: Viking Press, 1978.

Merton, Thomas. *The Way of Chuang Tzu.* New York: New Directions, 1965.

Merton, Thomas. *The Wisdom of the Desert.* New York: New Directions, 1960.

Monad, Jacques. *Chance and Necessity.* New York: Vintage 1972.

Naipaul, V. S. *Half a Life.* New York: Alfred A. Knopf, 2001.

Nietzsche, Friedrich. *The Gay Science.* Trans. Walter Kaufmann. New York: Vintage Books, 1974.

Nietzsche, Friedrich. *Thus Spoke Zarathustra.* Trans. Walter Kaufmann. New York: Viking Books, 1978.

Nishitani, Keiji. *Religion and Nothingness.* Trans. Jan Van Bragt. Berkeley: University of California Press, 1982.

Prigogine, Ilya and Isabelle Stingers. *Order Out of Chaos.* New York: Bantam, 1984.

Quinney, Richard. *Borderland: A Midwest Journal.* Madison: University of Wisconsin Press, 2001.

Quinney, Richard. *For the Time Being: Ethnography of Everyday Life.* Albany: State University Press of New York, 1998.

Quinney, Richard. *Journey to a Far Place: Autobiographical Reflections.* Philadelphia: Temple University Press, 1991.

Quinney, Richard. *Providence: The Reconstruction of Social and Moral Order.* New York: Longman, 1980.

Reps, Paul. *Zen Flesh, Zen Bones.* New York: Penguin, 1971.

Rilke, Rainer Maria. *Letters to a Young Poet.* Trans. Stephen Mitchell. Boston: Shambhala, 1993.

Rilke, Rainer Maria. *The Selected Poetry of Rainer Maria Rilke.* Ed. and trans. Stephen Mitchell. New York: Random House, 1982.

Seung Sahn. *Only Don't Know.* San Francisco: Four Seasons, 1982.

Shakespeare, William. *The Sonnets and Narrative Poems.* New York: Alfred A. Knopf, 1992.

Stegner, Wallace. *Where the Bluebird Sings to the Lemonade Springs.* New York: Random House, 1992.

Suzuki, Shunryu. *Zen Mind, Beginner's Mind.* New York: Weatherhill, 1970.

Tuan, Yi-Fu. *Space and Place.* Minneapolis: University of Minnesota Press, 1977.

Thoreau, Henry D. *Walden.* Ed. J. Lyndon Shanley. Princeton: Princeton University Press, 1973.

Vendler, Helen. *The Art of Shakespeare's Sonnets.* Cambridge: Harvard University Press, 1997.

Watts, Alan. *The Way of Liberation.* Ed. Mark Watts and Rebecca Shropshire. New York: Weatherhill, 1983.

Williams, William Carlos. *Paterson.* New York: New Directions, 1963.

Arthur M. Winfield (Edward Stratemeyer). *The Rover Boys at School.* Racine: Whitman Publishing, 1899.

Wittgenstein, Ludwig. *Tractatus Logico-Philosophicus.* Trans. C. K. Ogden. London: Routledge and Kegan Paul, 1981.

Wordsworth, William. *The Poems of William Wordsworth.* Ed. Jonathan Wordsworth. Cambridge, U.K.: University Printing House, 1973.

Wright, Charles. *The World of Ten Thousand Things, Poems 1980–1990.* New York: Farrar, Straus, and Giroux, 1990.

This book is set in Aldus roman, a typeface designed by Hermann Zapf and named for the fifteenth-century Venetian printer and publisher, Aldus Manutius. It was designed by Ken Crocker. The Stinehour Press printed the book on 70 lb. Cougar Opaque Natural Smooth paper. It was bound by Acme Bookbinding.